Recycled with Flair

Also by Ruth Stearns Egge

How to Make Something from Nothing

Recycled with Flair

How to Remodel Old Furniture
and Flea Market Finds

RUTH STEARNS EGGE

COWARD, McCANN & GEOGHEGAN, INC.
NEW YORK

 Published on the same day in Canada by Academic Press Canada Limited, Toronto.

Library of Congress Cataloging in Publication Data

Egge, Ruth Stearns.
Recycled with flair.

Includes index.
1. Furniture—Repairing. 2. Furniture finishing. I. Title.
TT199.E33 1980 684.1'044 79-19271
ISBN 0-698-11024-2
ISBN 0-698-11031-5 Pa.

Printed in the United States of America

Acknowledgments

I am deeply grateful to the many friends who offered encouragement and loaned me pieces to photograph.

A special acknowledgment to Shyrl, who constantly helped me move furniture. And to Bill Childers for his practical advice.

My warmest appreciation to Joe and Lois Hart who gave freely of their time and effort and to Betty Breitbarth for her generous help.

To the photographers who took the pictures for the book—Joe Egge, Michael Henley, Bill Hupp, Bruce Babb, Cecil Riley, Bill Rohrer and Jon, Jim and Jeanne Egge—a well-deserved thanks.

TO
NANCY, CINDEE, JEANNE,
JIM, JON AND JOE

Contents

Foreword

Some years back, when *new* meant nice and *old* was something nobody wanted, a lot of unattractive furniture—not to mention some we thought was ugly that wasn't—found its way into attics and basements and secondhand stores.

Today these relics are being given another go-around, and a new hobby has sprung up whereby yesterday's discards are turned into handsome furnishings for our homes. A by-product of this newfound interest is recycling the leftover parts and pieces. The most outlandish table, cabinet or cupboard (broken or otherwise) can provide the amateur hobbyist with whole sections of prefabricated material—an unbeatable shortcut for do-it-yourself projects.

This book will help you discover for yourself how easy it is to make over such castoffs to suit your own particular tastes, your pocketbook and your life-style.

Part One

The Before and After Story

1

Creative Ways to Reclaim Old Furniture and Salvage

"If you want something done right, do it yourself," my grandmother used to say. To her, I'm sure the proverb really meant, "Do it yourself so you can have it *your way*—and *save money* besides." And grandmother did love a bargain.

But don't we all! Take the young college student I talked with at the bus stop last week who was so pleased over a marvelous buy found at a garage sale. He'd paid a dollar for an ugly green bookcase and discovered later, when the paint was stripped off, that it was a solid maple piece from the thirties.

Or the man I met recently who told me he attended a farm sale in the Midwest and invested twenty-five dollars in a broken-down cupboard that he eventually repaired and sold for several times its original cost. Naturally, such finds are rare, and all bargains are not antiques. But one woman I know visited a San Francisco flea market in search of cast-off furniture to remodel and carted home a

Plate 1: Wall piece built by Betty Breitbarth, Portland, Oregon, for Mrs. Ward Zea, West Linn, Oregon.

secondhand dresser. She cut it down into a low chest, hung a tall mirror salvaged from another sale above it and finished the whole thing in antique red to complement her daughter's room. The results were smashing!

Another friend of mine, after pondering the remains of an estate sale, rescued two derelict tables that were left in the attic and transformed them with paint and ingenuity into an elegant piece for her entry hall.

As any treasure hunter can tell you, this is all part of the game—whether you dig for Spanish silver or look through barns and dusty shops for ruins of antiques. The excitement of refurbishing your finds gives added zest to

Plate 2: Composite cupboard by Betty Breitbarth, Portland, Oregon.

any hunt for salvage, and when it comes to that—and to knowing what to do with things after you've found them—I can tell you about a woman who is hard to beat.

Betty Breitbarth, of Portland, Oregon, makes over all sorts of relics, including furniture. For her, it is pure pleasure when she can take castoffs that have gathered scars of neglect for years and make them beautiful again or put them to new use.

Her home is furnished with things she has recycled. The wall piece in Plate 1 she made from bits and parts of old furniture. Some of these parts were remnants of antiques that had been deeply colored with red mahogany stain. Since this was impossible to remove, she combined the antique parts with scraps of other wood and painted the entire wall shelf a mellow golden tone, antiqued to resemble natural wood.

She fashioned the handsome piece in Plate 2 from a remodeled chest. The lower drawers were broken so in their place she added doors and on top of the chest put a cast-off cupboard. For missing glass in the cupboard's doors she substituted hardboard panels with hand-painted designs.

Another woman of great imagination, Bernice Fields, owns a small shop in a western city. She buys and sells antiques, but what really brings the customers flocking to her store are the pieces she designs from odds and ends of old wood, broken parts of antiques, and secondhand furniture. She haunts the auctions, flea markets and sales, on the lookout for anything and everything that can be rebuilt or redone. Once she has studied the possibilities and decided what to do with each purchase, her designs are put together by a retired handyman. After this, Mrs. Fields stains, paints, refinishes and does whatever is necessary to give them a finished look. She then sells them at modest prices with no pretense of their being authentic antiques.

Of course, they aren't copies either, because while the materials salvaged from many sources determine what the overall style will be, each desk, stand or cupboard is one of a kind, different in some way from all the others. What sets her pieces apart even more, I think, is a certain air of mellowness that stems, possibly, from the aged wood used in their construction. Mrs. Fields agrees, and points out that if she were to buy all new material instead of incorporating old things into her furniture and accessory designs, the pieces would then acquire a store-bought look—one her customers would not find so appealing.

Basically, her concept simply carries one step further something antique dealers have *always* known: that when antiques are broken, or parts of them are missing, you don't throw them away. You improvise—find similar parts to replace whatever is gone. Thus, when you're working with parts that are old, the end result may be a "marriage of antiques." Once you begin to explore what can be done with things that are not so old too, and once you go beyond the thought of simply repairing, then you have *creative furniture.*

The secret of Mrs. Fields' success, I'm sure, is her willingness to apply improbable ideas to the most unlikely pieces. When she looks for possibilities in a cast-off chest, table or even a bit of hardware, she does so with an open mind.

At an auction, I once saw her buy an unattractive chest that brought only a few scattered bids—because there weren't many buyers with the vision to realize that, underneath its glaring Formica-like finish and angular metal trim, was a truly delightful piece of furniture; a deep, commodious chest with a drawer below, cedar lined and sweet smelling.

I dropped in to see Mrs. Fields a week later. She had stripped off the ugly lacquer, toned down the wood with household bleach, covered over the metal trim with a

Plate 3: Dictionary stand designed by Bernice Fields, Portland, Oregon, utilizes parts of secondhand furniture.

Plate 4: Small pedestal desk built by Bernice Fields, Portland, Oregon, is used as a nightstand in the home of Jon and Nancy Egge, Milwaukie, Oregon.

wooden molding and given the entire chest a waxed oil finish.

Among the other items that Mrs. Fields bought at this same auction were eleven small tables in varying stages of disrepair, possibly from an apartment house destined for the wreckers. Although the tables contained some good building parts, they were all either too badly damaged or else not attractive enough to be desirable. And as Mrs. Fields said, "If I had left them the way they were, I'd have had them sitting around my shop forever." Instead, she turned them into a variety of useful and interesting pieces.

The base for the book stand in Plate 3 came from one of these tables, and so did the little desk in Plate 4.

When economy is of prime importance, it becomes a challenge to see what you can do with inexpensive salvage and castoffs.

Take the wall piece in Plate 5, which I assembled from odds and ends gathered at garage and rummage sales. For a painted piece such as this, parts from many sources will blend harmoniously. Often you can buy this kind of material for pennies—more about this later. A limited budget need not stifle creativity.

Grandmother, practical as she was, found time to contrive small touches of beauty for her home. Quite apart from the pleasure of owning beautiful things and what they can add to your life, think of the *fun* of being able to put together your own accessories: decorator pieces you might not feel you could afford to buy—a plant stand to show off your favorite fern, a handcrafted wedding gift or a wall piece to hold candles for a special party. It satisfies some deep creative urge when you can translate into reality something you want for your home. If you can do it inexpensively with your own two hands and breathe new life into what otherwise might be considered junk, that is truly rewarding!

Plate 5: White wall piece by the author from odds and ends. Accessories include a blue and white figurine, flowered platter and teapot.

Creative Ways to Reclaim Old Furniture and Salvage

Many of the world's happiest discoveries have been made through *serendipity,* the finding of one thing while you look for another. Who knows what treasures—or talents—you may uncover once you let yourself go.

2

You Can Do It—How and Where to Begin

Long ago, when furniture styles were born in the courts of kings, elaborate designs of the day were modified as peasants and tradesmen built furniture to suit themselves—simple cupboards, chests and tables for their cottages or country kitchens. Gradually, there emerged a whole new style. Thus were created some of the lovely provincial pieces that still survive today.

Aside from expensive finely crafted furnishings, what will remain of our own tastes and times? A hundred years from now, will people be collecting plastic-fronted furniture or will they find more pleasure in the less-than-perfect kind of thing that you and I might put together to please ourselves?

Like those peasants of days gone by, why not create your own environment? Go looking for things to transform, and make them over to suit your style of living; it can become a do-it-yourself venture with all the excitement of a treasure hunt.

How Do You Start?

Let's take one or two items you might run across, then think about what can be done with them.

If you like the "antique look," there are still parts of mirror frames from old dressers or chiffoniers around. (Often the mirror itself and sometimes the frame will be gone, but the supports, or easel, from which the mirror was suspended will turn up in a sale somewhere.) Although in the past these easels have been plentiful and inexpensive, there is currently a trend on the part of dealers to attach them to old chests and dressers.

In actual use, a mirror suspended in this fashion is less

Plate 6: Plant alcove featuring plant stand and hanging planters by the author, table by Mrs. John Moore.

Plate 7: Coatrack by the author is recycled mirror support shown "before" in Plate 8.

Plate 8: Broken mirror support.

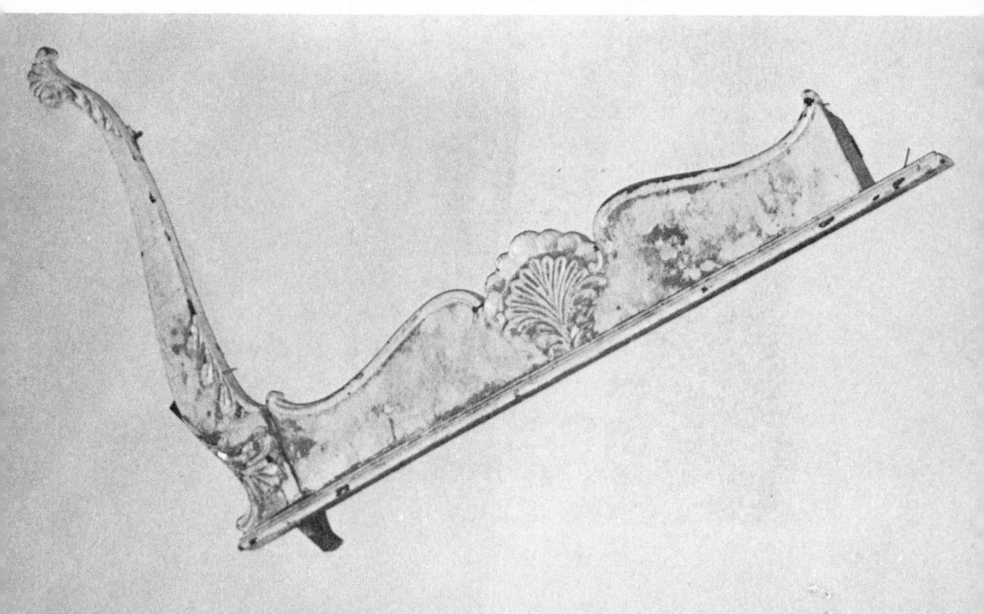

than satisfactory because it tends to tilt unexpectedly too far forward or back; nor is this type of mirror as flexible from a decorating standpoint as one that hangs on the wall. So I predict that we'll be seeing a lot of these old mirror supports being sold once again as leftover parts or pretty pieces of wood.

Here are a couple of ways you can use these supports. Plate 6 shows one made into a narrow table for a plant alcove. It could also enhance an entrance hall.In Plate 7, part of an easel is converted into a coatrack. Further on in this chapter I'll tell you exactly how it was done. (It is pictured *"before"* in Plate 8.)

When you are making the rounds of the thrift stores and you see a piece of secondhand furniture, consider its best features and its worst. Does it have potential as a piece of furniture? Is it worth buying for parts? For example, this is how you might sum up the little sewing cabinet in Plate 9.

Assets	***Liabilities***
Convenient height	Ugly drawer pulls
Handy divided drawers	Poor finish
Reasonable price	Spindly legs

Ask yourself, *How do I utilize the drawers, but make them more attractive?* Sawing off the spindly legs is not a solution because your cabinet would then become a sewing box and you'd sacrifice one asset—its height.

Where Do You Get Ideas?

So what *do* you do? Your mind starts reaching out for possibilities: This is the kind of springboard that makes you think creatively. For instance, you'll look at every piece of furniture or secondhand castoff from a different perspective, mentally noting whether or not it might yield something you can combine with the sewing cabinet's

Plate 9: "Before" photo of three-drawer sewing cabinet, shown recycled in Plate 10.

Plate 10: Display cabinet by the author combines part of a three-drawer sewing cabinet (Plate 9) and part of an old phonograph cabinet, shown "before" in Diagram 12. Accessories by Peggy Baxter and Nancy Egge.

drawers. In the back of your mind too will be the matter of hardware to replace the ugly pulls. Things you see in stores or in people's homes will suggest an idea. And each idea will trigger more.

The display-cabinet/drawer combination in Plate 10 shows how the sewing cabinet's liabilities were eventually minimized and its good features retained. Yet *your* remodeling ideas for the sewing cabinet—or someone else's—might be entirely different. That is the beautiful part of do-it-yourself tailoring your furnishings to suit you.

Another way to spark ideas is to channel your thinking toward some particular piece of furniture; you might have a yen for a large dining-room cupboard, for example. There is much to be said for this single-minded approach. You'll tend to look at everything with an eye to adapting it for that cupboard, and when you run across old furniture (even parts and pieces), you will mentally note any similarity in line or design to the piece you have in mind. You'll immediately begin to visualize how this or that would look cut down, painted, rebuilt—perhaps with a section removed here, a decoration added there.

It's as simple as that. So never, never say you haven't any imagination. And when it comes to the actual remodeling, that needn't scare you either.

Shortcuts

There is one definite advantage that *rebuilding* has over building from scratch: it provides you with prefabricated material so you achieve results more *quickly*.

In the beginning, the more you can utilize ready-built portions of old or castoff furniture, the easier the rebuilding process will be. Even so, it's necessary to muddle through a bit at first until you get the feel of it. And there is much to be said for the theory of "learning by doing."

Plate 11: Revolving dictionary stand assembled by Betty Breitbarth, Portland, Oregon.

For instance, as you study ways to use preconstructed parts and become aware of how they were put together in the first place, you'll automatically absorb a good bit of construction "know-how" along with basic principles of building. And your ideas and designs will move ahead accordingly.

As an example, take the book stand in Plate 11. It utilizes the ball-bearing mechanism from a lazy Susan. I have since discovered an easier way to make these book stands using tiny rollers from the hardware store. But if I hadn't first taken apart a lazy Susan and pondered what to do with it, the idea of a revolving book stand might never have occurred to me.

One Step at a Time

The key to utilizing parts and pieces of ready-made furniture is step-at-a-time construction. Thus you solve each problem as it comes along. Besides, when you work with prefabricated and secondhand material it is more or less uncharted territory anyway, and each project is bound to present different problems.

If you make a mistake, it is no great thing. Because the next step simply becomes finding a way to correct it—possibly with ornamentation, or by altering your design to compensate.

It may well be that an amateur is better suited to this kind of building than a skilled craftsman—since the do-it-yourselfer learns to work by trial and error and therefore is willing to experiment and move ahead a step at a time, while the carpenter who knows his trade would rather proceed in an orderly way.

Tools and Equipment

If you have access to, and can use, power saws and a drill press, it will make building that much easier. However, except for an occasional carpenter-cut board, all of the projects included here were assembled using ordinary hand tools—with one exception, an *electric drill.* This I think is almost a necessity since most of the pieces are put together with glue and screws, rather than nails. For this learn-as-you-go type of construction—where you work along a step at a time and aren't quite sure what the next step will be—a nail in the wrong place can mean split wood, not to mention the pounding which could knock your entire project apart before you have it together.

On the other hand, when you attach one piece of wood to another with a drilled hole and a screw, and it turns out wrong, you can simply remove the screw, fill the hole with putty and start over.

A common mistake is drilling either too large a hole so the screw does not hold well or so small a one that's difficult to tighten. However, this method of building becomes easy once you learn which drill bit is the right diameter for a particular size of screw. The chart at the end of this chapter gives diameters and comparative sizes of both bits and screws.

With an electric drill, you can accomplish wonders. But observe ordinary safety precautions such as not wearing loose, billowy clothing that could catch in the drill; remembering to grip firmly or clamp in a vise any board in which you're drilling a hole; and making a small hole with the point of a nail or an awl before you start drilling so that the drill will stay on course. And always unplug the drill while changing bits.

A *wood rasp* is one thing I couldn't do without. You can use it for rounding edges and corners to achieve some remarkably finished effects. A vise is also an invaluable aid. As for glue, epoxy can be used occasionally where a thicker glue with more body is needed, but in most cases, gluing can be done either with white all-purpose glue or Elmer's Carpenter's Wood Glue.

In cases where you're unsure of the particular tool you

may need, ask your hardware store man. I've always found them to be very helpful.

Checklist of Tools and Supplies

Screws in assorted sizes
Brads and small finishing nails
White all-purpose, or Elmer's wood glue
Epoxy glue
Screwdrivers
Pliers
Vise
Drill (preferably electric)
Drill bits (in assorted sizes)
Hammer
Wood chisels
Sandpaper
Wood rasp—the large lightweight kind with a handle
Square
Paint (as needed)
Clamps
Saws (smaller sizes are more useful)

If you're really set on having something a particular way, don't be too quick to accept an expert's opinion that "it can't be done." Perhaps it can't if you follow all the rules. But I've seen some lovely, original pieces turned out by do-it-yourselfers with nothing more going for them than their own determination to translate into reality something they've envisioned in their minds. A wall piece I've seen illustrates this point since its construction violates a basic rule of carpentry—that two boards should not be glued together end to end. Plain end-butt joints, because they are structurally weak, are considered taboo.

The woman who built the piece didn't go by the rules,

and therefore managed to accomplish what she wanted. Of course a decorative piece such as this allows much latitude for cover-ups and reinforcing, but the point is, if she had felt bound to "go by the book," her idea might have been discarded before it was tried. Remember, creative thinking can be as simple as having the courage to take off in new directions. And an amateur may have the advantage of being less inhibited by rules and patterns of thought than a professional.

Think! Plan! Do!

After you've acquired a little confidence, you may want to polish your skills. But at first, if you become preoccupied with following a lot of construction dos and don'ts, the whole thing begins to look too complicated. Instead, think about your project in odd moments while you are doing other things. You needn't anticipate beforehand what each step will be, but do consider what materials might work best and try to plan what you will do *first.* By thinking about a project ahead of time, you often improve on your original idea. Once you start, a single inspiration or thought will lead logically to others, until before you know it you'll have a workable plan.

Here's one example of how an idea gradually evolves if you give it time. The plant alcove in Plate 6 was a project I thought about for weeks. And this may have eliminated some of the mistakes in my earlier plan.

It started with a picture I saw in a magazine showing indoor plants grouped in a window garden. Since all the windows in our house open inward and have radiators beneath them, I settled for an alcove in the dining room. Which of course meant I'd need artificial light for the plants.

That brought up another problem. With the archway open in front and nothing to screen it, a fluorescent light would be glaringly obvious. Could I conceal it with a curtain? Or a valance? On a curve, these might prove difficult.

Next, I considered various kinds and heights of shutters. And then the idea of using the headboard from an old bed came to me. I was sure that was it—until I measured the alcove and realized it was a few inches wider than even a king-size bed. (I'll remember the headboard, though, as an idea to use in some other place.)

Eventually, I had a carpenter make me a cornice board, after I'd drawn the curves I wanted and cut a half-pattern from a folded strip of butcher's paper so that both ends would be exactly the same.

One more thing: save magazine and newspaper drawings, or photographs of furnishings that appeal to you and study furniture displays in the store. It gives form and substance to your ideas if you staple or tape pictures into a notebook.

For instance, an ad in a magazine for ready-to-assemble wall shelves suggested one way to use a legless tabletop by turning it into the wall-hung desk shown in Plate 12.

For the coatrack that I told you about earlier (Plate 7), you can use part of an old mirror easel as I did, or any nicely shaped board of similar size. The same construction would apply and, as mentioned, an antique effect can be achieved with paint and inexpensive materials. We'll go into more detail on this in later chapters.

For recycling the easel shown in Plate 8, I used the following method.

Coatrack

Step 1: Preparing the Board. Remove the remaining sidepiece of the easel. Strip off old paint with paint remover as recommended in Chapter 13. Then, with a

Plate 12: Broken table recycled by Betty Breitbarth becomes a wall-hung desk/buffet.

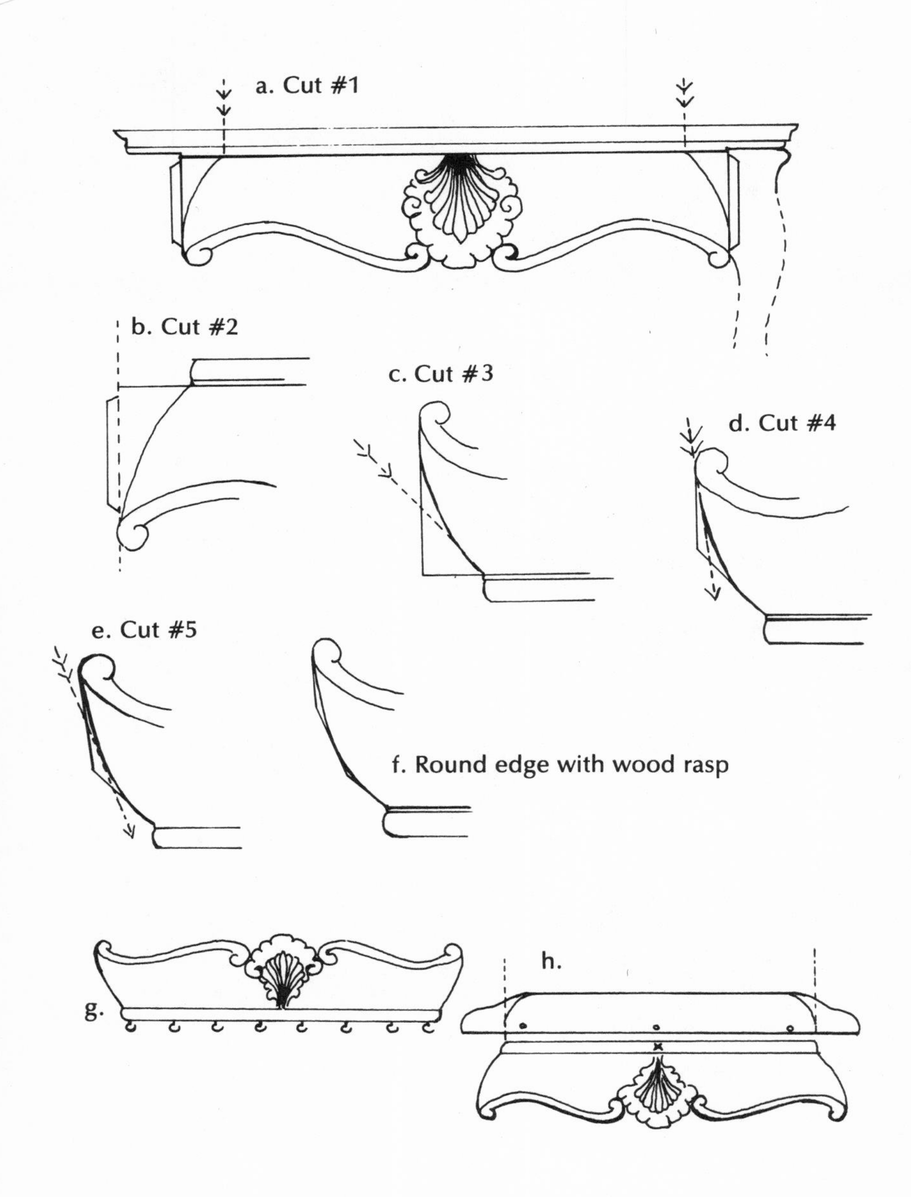

Diagram 1

soft pencil, draw approximate curve on the board. Diagram 1.

Next, clamp board in vise (with molding at top), but protect it with a couple of scrap pieces of wood clamped one on either side—to keep the jaws of the vise from making indentations.

Note: Reverse position of board in vise as necessary, (see diagrams). And, as you finish drawing a line or making a cut on one end of board, repeat it on the other so curves on both ends will match.

Step 2: Cutting the Curves. Cut #1 (Diagram 1a). Saw off ends of molding along dotted lines to point where curves intersect the molding. Round the cut ends with wood rasp and sand smooth. Cut #2 (Diagram 1b). Saw off projections on ends of board. Cut #3 (Diagram 1c). Draw a straight line across corner ending at junction of curve and molding. Saw off corner. Cut #4 (Diagram 1d). Draw a straight line from outer edge of curlicue to intersect Cut #3 as shown in diagram. Cut #5 (Diagram 1e). Draw a line (as illustrated in diagram) to eliminate angle. Saw off point.

Step 3: Rounding the Edges. With board clamped firmly in vise, use wood rasp to round cut edges, moving toward the center of edge from both back and front sides of the board—and carefully along center ridge until curve becomes rounded and fairly smooth. Diagram 1f.

Sand with coarse, then fine, sandpaper.

Note: Never dispose of any ornamentation from old furniture; even the tiniest piece can be useful. I'll tell you more about how to shape and adapt these as we work along.

Step 4: Finishing. Rub oil into the board—either Danish oil or a mixture of half linseed oil and half turpentine. Rub in well and wipe off excess.

At this point, all that's needed is a pair of coat hooks, (old ones or reproductions) and the coatrack will look quite finished, with or without the addition of a shelf. I attached a shelf simply because I happened to have an oak board that seemed just right for this particular piece. If you are going to include a shelf, add the hooks last.

Step 5: Adding a Shelf. Since my shelf board was at least 10 inches longer than the coatrack, the ends had to be cut off. To do this, match center of shelf to center of the molding on the coatrack board. Diagram 1h. Mark and saw off the ends, round the edges with a rasp and sand with coarse, then fine sandpaper.

Clamp shelf in vise (with piece of scrap wood on each side to protect it). Using an $^{11}/_{64}$-inch bit, drill three holes in shelf at points indicated in Diagram 1h.

If you'll look at the chart on page 45, you will see that a 1-inch No. 8 screw will slip easily into this size hole. Also according to the chart, the threaded part of the screw, which must be firmly imbedded in the molding on the coatrack, will require a $^{3}/_{32}$-inch bit to drill the pilot hole.

Now counterbore each of the three pilot holes in the shelf with a $^{5}/_{16}$-inch bit, so the screw head can be set down into the wood and concealed with a plug (cut from a wooden dowel).

Note: Countersink bits in various sizes are available at hardware stores, and are specifically designed for recessing the head of the screw. There are also three-in-one bits that drill a hole for the thread and the shank, countersink and counterbore in one operation. Or you can follow the chart and do it this way:

After you've drilled a pilot hole, change your drill bit to one that is slightly larger than the head of the screw you plan to use. Then drill again in the same hole—but only for about ⅛ inch into the wood—just enough to *countersink* the head of the screw below the surface. To *counterbore,* drill a little deeper so there will be room to insert a wooden plug that will cover the head of the screw. (For illustration of these terms, see charts on page 45.)

Before fastening the shelf to the coatrack with three 1-inch No. 8 screws, sand then oil shelf on both sides. Wipe thoroughly. Give entire coatrack another light application of oil after shelf is attached, the screws are tightened and the wooden plugs are in place.

Step 6: Hanging the Coatrack. Here is one way you can hang a heavy oak piece such as this.

I used two "saw tooth" picture hangers (available in various sizes at hardware stores), one near each end of the coatrack board. While these particular hangers are quite sturdy, the nails that come with them are much too small for a wall piece with any weight.

In adapting these hangers to the coatrack, I replaced the nails with short (⅝-inch) No. 4 screws after I'd enlarged existing holes in the end of each hanger. To make the holes bigger, grip one end of the metal hanger firmly in a pair of pliers while you drill (with a ⅛-inch bit) through the tiny hole at the other end into a piece of scrap wood clamped securely to your workbench.

As the chart shows, you'll need 1/16-inch holes in the back of the board for attaching the hangers with the No. 4 screws.

To hang the coatrack, pound two 1-inch flat head nails (roofing nails are fine) into the wall. Large flat nail heads hold well against the metal teeth of these sawtoothed hangers, so let the heads project just enough for the hangers to slip over them.

Note: Even when a piece is not large, a single hanger in the center is not adequate for any shelf that may be unbalanced by objects placed on it, or for a coatrack which may be unequally loaded. This is why two hangers were fastened to the back of the coatrack, one on each end. Sometimes, instead of using sawtoothed hangers, a wall piece may be hung by means of tautly stretched, heavy picture wire attached to its back with two good-sized screw eyes which are countersunk—so they're level with the surface of the wood. But for some coatracks and bulletin boards the most satisfactory method of hanging them is to drill a couple of holes in the backboard itself, then fasten securely to the wall with screws.

Alternative Ideas for Coatrack Board

You might prefer the board turned the other way up with a coat hook at each end. Or, with small hooks along the bottom edge, it could be used as a key rack (Diagram 1g).

In times past, when handcrafting was a way of life, every man's home was made to his order. Hopefully, our time too will be remembered as an age when creativity flourished, and old crafts and skills were relearned.

CHART FOR COMPARATIVE SIZES OF DRILL BITS AND SCREWS

	Number	Number	Number	Number	Number	Number
Most commonly used sizes of flat head screws	4	6	8	10	12	14
Size of hole for shank of screw — Screw should fit easily into hole	1⁄8	5⁄32	11⁄64	13⁄64	15⁄64	1⁄4
Size of hole for threaded end of screw — Threaded end must be firmly imbedded in wood, so pilot hole is smaller	1⁄16	1⁄16	3⁄32	7⁄64	1⁄8	9⁄64
To countersink head of screw—just enough to putty over	15⁄64 (Drill shallow hole)	17⁄64	19⁄64	3⁄8	13⁄32	29⁄64
To counterbore (sink below surface and cover with wooden plug)	1⁄4	9⁄32	5⁄16	25⁄64	27⁄64	15⁄32

3

The Art of Salvage

I was revisiting a turn-of-the-century home. The old-time feel of that house, with its own stories built right in, took me back a hundred years—no matter that I'd never been there. Not until later did I learn that the place had been built only eighteen years before. It had been designed by a man who loved the mellow look of old things and had salvaged windows, doors, woodwork and hardware from long-ago buildings in the United States and abroad.

Stained glass windows were highlights of each bath; oak bookcases had been built into the walls; curved balusters added to the stairs. The place was comfortable, softly glowing with carved wood, old copper and brass.

Of course, when it comes to old treasures, we also think of sky-high prices. Obviously, this home was an expensive project, far beyond the average budget. I came away from the house thinking how beautiful it was. And how costly.

Some weeks later, I stopped in to see a friend whose home, though far from being so elaborate, has the same gentle air of old-time charm. In this house, certainly there has never been lavish expenditure on antiques. But it is full of chests and tables and drawers—cherished pieces—redone or made over with just an echo of nostalgia. As one well-known decorator says, "Good decorating may simply be the art of producing a *mood* through use of imagination."

Surely if we can capture a flavor of times past without insisting every detail be authentic, it puts the whole idea of salvage in a more reasonable light. And anyone can learn to use salvage creatively, to transform old things—new ones too—in a hundred different ways, and for a good deal less money. Make no mistake about it—*junking* has become a respectable art, with everyone from students to bankers looking for bargains.

What to Look for and Where to Find It

Because antiques are presently at a premium, it is a constant surprise to me when I find odds, ends and parts of prize pieces still around. You won't of course happen onto such things as carved wood or antiques—or even parts of them—every day. But if you keep looking in all the places I'm going to tell you about, you're bound to discover a few now and then—that I can promise you. Prices will vary; some may leave you breathless, but once in a while you'll happen onto an excellent bargain.

One peculiar thing about buying: cost is always relative. Just a few weeks ago I neglected to buy an old mirror frame covered with attic dust that was priced at only a dollar—surely a good buy. Yet it seemed to me at the time hardly worth the trouble to carry it—dusty as it was—down a flight of stairs and out to the car. You will find there are days when you'd consider such a bargain well worth the effort and other days when you're almost too selective for your own good.

Some pieces you may decide to leave just as they are, or refinish only. Personally, I can't bear to paint a good hardwood piece of furniture. Nor can I bring myself to take apart one that is reasonably solid and attractive.

The ones you will look for to make over or rebuild are those it would be impractical to restore—perhaps because they are unattractive, or have been damaged beyond repair, or because there are too many parts missing.

And you wouldn't believe the things people have done to fine old furniture in the name of convenience. I found the lovely oak table legs (Plate 13) in a rural Grange hall. Although the entire table was solid oak, it had been used as a cutting board and to hold hot dishes so that the top was irreparably scarred. By way of support, rough boards had been nailed crisscross with 3-inch spikes from the underside of the tabletop to each leg. But even with all this abuse, the skirting around the top, as well as the legs and some of the assembly mechanism (glides and so on) were salvageable.

I thought the legs so handsome that I tracked down a member of the local Grange who was custodian of the building, and he sold me the table for a few dollars. To clinch the bargain, I gave the members a table I had in my basement—a sturdy, Formica-topped affair that was better suited to their needs.

If only I had a dollar for every ruined table and chest of drawers I've seen with the legs sawed off a couple of inches, or sometimes more—but just enough to look amateurishly "done over." Although I hate to admit it, I've ruined a few myself in early saw-happy attempts to "modernize" family hand-me-downs. A favorite project of mine now is the transformation of old furniture with

Plate 13: Curved oak legs salvaged from a table with ruined top.

Plate 14: "Before" photo of oak table with sawed-off legs and missing top (used upside down as a base in Plate 40).

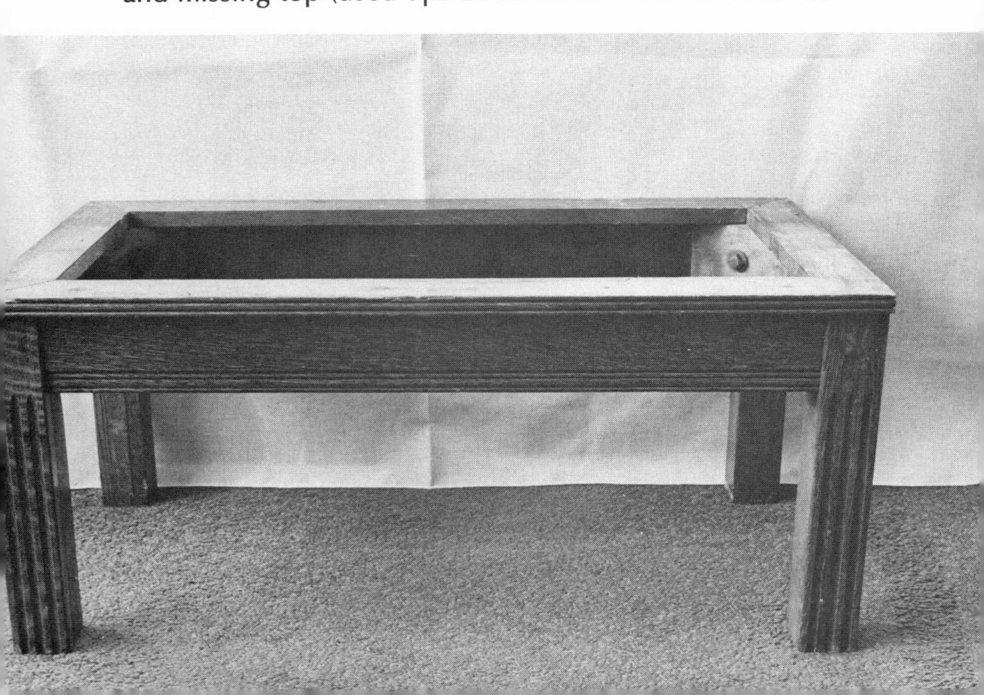

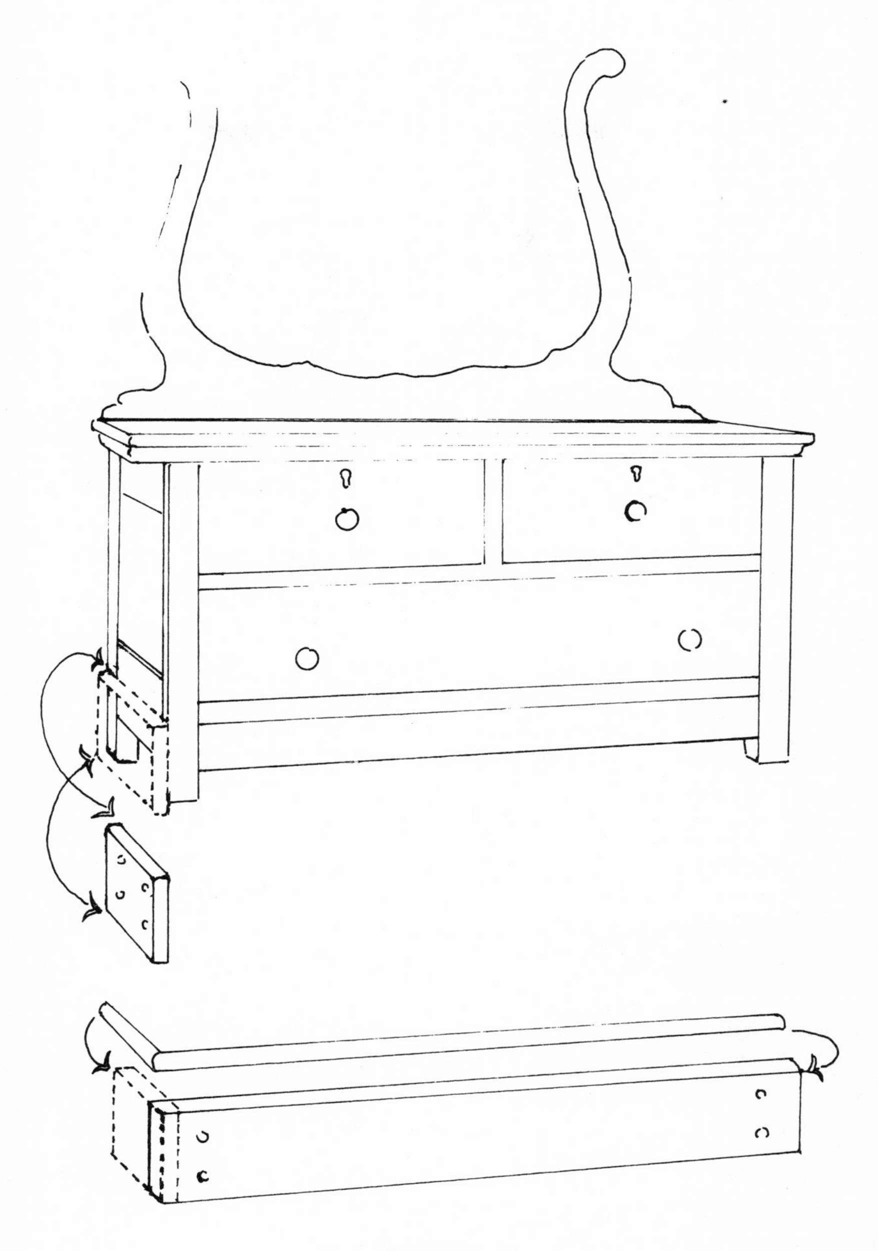

Diagram 2

cutoff legs. Examples of such pieces are pictured "before" in Plate 14, and in Diagram 2.

Other items to look for are bits of metal and brass or cast-iron hardware left over from long-forgotten relics.

Farm, Secondhand and Antique Auctions

I bought a pair of lovely oversized handles along with a boxful of knobs, drawer pulls and old trunk hardware for three dollars at a *country auction.* Most of the items in the box, including the handles, had been through a fire, which meant they would have to be plated or painted, and this was probably the reason I got them so cheaply.

This particular auction was held in a community hall and drew a standing-room-only crowd. Midway through the proceedings, everyone trooped outdoors to follow the auctioning of a truck, a Shetland pony and a palomino. Then back into the hall went the spectators and auctioneer as bidding continued on guns, tools and a variety of household items. Just inside the front door was a big open-topped box with a sign, FREE KITTENS. Late in the day, I heard their owner complain that he had two more kittens than when he started. During the afternoon, someone had slipped a couple of extras into the box.

Auctions are great fun, partly because they generate an air of excitement. And it's contagious! Beware of getting caught up in it if you've never attended one. You can, however, be overly cautious. I once let a massive 6-foot oak mirror frame go by when the bidding reached fifty-five dollars because I lost my nerve and thought, that's too high! Apparently, it wasn't; I saw the frame a week later in an antique show priced at exactly a hundred dollars more.

One important rule of auction-going is to be sure you know and want what you are getting. Look over the merchandise beforehand. Most auctions are open either on the day of the sale or earlier, so you can preview what will be sold. Ads in the paper usually mention viewing hours. Take a tape measure along when you preview, as well as a small notebook to list descriptions and identifying code numbers. When auction-time arrives, use it for jotting down final bids and what you bought.

Decide ahead of time how much you are willing to pay for a particular piece. To get a better perspective on this, visualize the item sitting in an antique store with a price tag on it. Then, in your own mind, set a limit—what it is worth to you.

When it comes to prices, you can expect, as a rule, to pay less at an auction than in a store, because dealers who buy at auction (and all of them do) must allow for markup. Thus an ardent collector will often bid higher, putting the dealer, who hopes to make a profit, at a disadvantage. On the other hand, the dealer usually has a far more realistic knowledge of prices and value, and this tends to even the odds.

You can sometimes buy the larger pieces of furniture—built when ceilings were high and rooms were big—at bargain prices. And these offer excellent possibilities for restyling. However, unless you can arrange for delivery, better concentrate on smaller items.

You'll acquire a feel for auction-going after you've attended a few. So go early to get a good seat, and stay, if you can, until it is over. Often the best buys are to be had near the end, when people grow tired and start leaving. You will find it easier too, after the crowd thins out, to watch and learn, and get the feel of bidding.

Warehouse and Storage Auctions; Estate Auctions

Unless the newspaper ad specifically states "furniture" (or whatever it is you are looking for), warehouse and storage auctions can be a waste of time. Although you may find an occasional piece of furniture, or lamps that may be useful for parts, this type of auction is more apt to be a grab-bag sort of thing where you bid on boxes or barrels of household goods without much idea of what you're getting. My husband attended one such sale because a friend of his had paid fifty dollars at a warehouse auction for a barrel of dishes worth two hundred dollars. With the exception of one silver tray, however, the barrel my husband brought home (for twenty-five dollars) was filled to the brim with junk.

Bidding is usually brisk at *estate auctions.* Here again, go early and study the merchandise, since these auctions attract collectors and dealers—as do auctions that specialize in contents and furnishings from old buildings, apartment houses or hotels that are going to be torn down.

Garage Sales—by Any Other Name

In rural or suburban areas, garage sales—also called house, tag, patio, basement, attic, yard, or miscellaneous sales—can be excellent sources of material. (I try to concentrate on those nearby, except for an occasional well-publicized sale.)

Tops in this category is the *estate sale,* because you're more apt to find antiques at a reasonable price—except at an occasional sale where you'll find them priced clear out of sight by individuals who are out of touch with current trends and think an antique is worth any amount they want to ask.

Here again, the secret is to get there early. If you wait, all the goodies will be gone because dealers make the rounds too. They often read the ads in the evening edition of the next day's paper and get there when the sale starts—or before.

However, anyone can play this game, and it's a lot of fun. Start by checking the ads each day under three headings: Miscellaneous, Antiques and Garage Sales. It's a good idea to read through them even if you are not going to any sales that day because it keeps you abreast of the market. You'll be aware then of ads that are reruns and can pick out those that are new and current.

The method that works best for me is to go through the paper and note the sales in my general locality. I then circle the ads, or tape them to a sheet of paper (grouping them together by street numbers and addresses) and write the addresses plainly alongside, so they are easy to see while I'm driving without my glasses. It is advantageous to attend a lot of sales, even though you don't always buy, so you'll know which items are bargains and which ones are not.

A lot of really fine stuff is dug out of attics, garages and basements along with the trash. This unknown quantity is, perhaps, why garage and estate sales are so interesting. If you are persevering, you are apt to uncover some treasures.

At this kind of sale, particularly if it's professionally conducted, numbers may be issued to customers as they arrive. Then at the appointed hour, anywhere from ten to twenty-five people are admitted at a time. However, if the ad states 9:00 A.M. you can go an hour or more ahead of time. Rap on the door to receive your numbered ticket; come back when the sale starts (exactly at nine) and wait for your number to be called.

A professionally conducted sale offers certain other advantages. If you are timid about going into neighborhoods you don't know, these sales are well supervised and may even have a uniformed guard on the premises. Also, on a weekend sale or those that run more than one day, the merchandise is often marked down on the last day. At a typical sale in this area (West Coast), for instance, if the sale runs Saturday and Sunday, from nine to five, any item in the twenty-dollars-or-under category that has not been sold by one o'clock Sunday afternoon will be marked down one-third. At three o'clock it will be reduced to half price. However, sales go strictly by the rules. So don't carry the merchandise around ahead of time or you might find yourself paying full price.

It is practically impossible to quote prices since they can change in a matter of weeks and vary in different localities. As a basis for comparison, however, a sorry-looking table with a ruined top was offered at a sale for fifteen dollars the first day—more than I felt it was worth to me. But because the sale was in the immediate neighborhood, and there didn't appear to be a great deal of interest shown in it, I optimistically waited past the one o'clock markdown. I was at the cash register, money in hand, at three o'clock to buy the table for seven-fifty, bringing along my pliers and screwdriver to disassemble it. Not too bad a buy when you consider that the salvageable parts included two sets of preassembled oak legs.

A portion of the tabletop—the part that wasn't warped—was also worth saving, as were the fifty-year-old locking mechanism and a set of hardwood table glides. The last two items could be traded to an antique dealer should I decide not to use them myself.

Thrift Stores

Not too long ago I would have said that thrift stores might be your best bet so far as material is concerned. In cities of any size, these are still a fairly good source. But unless you are there when the trucks come in—and this means inquiring ahead as to which day and what time—you may not find these stores too productive.

However, there are people who make it a point to be at, for example, the Red and White thrift store at nine o'clock Tuesday morning or twelve o'clock Thursday or whatever time the truck is unloading. This frequently pays off in their finding some good furniture or other salvage. Often, prices are a bit lower then too—particularly if you're able to take your purchase with you since they won't then have to store or move it around.

The Old, the New and the In-betweens

To summarize, here is a sampling of what you may want to look for:

OLD

Parts and Pieces of Old Furniture:

Mirrors and frames (also hardwood picture frames)
Mirror easels
Cupboard crowns
Fancy moldings
Bits of carved wood or gingerbread
Dresser pediments
Legs
Bases
Drawer pulls (of wood, brass, cast iron or whatever)
Baluster posts (small or large)
Ornate or plain metal hardware of all kinds (back plates, escutcheons and so on)
Fancy cast iron (from old stoves, heating registers, etc.)
Thin boards that aren't plywood (useful for backing or drawer bottoms)
Pieces of oak or other hardwood
Tabletops
Small occasional tables
Glass doors and wooden doors

Salvage from Old Buildings:

Exterior and interior gingerbread
Hardwood boards and moldings
Plinth blocks (these framed old doorways)

Porch-railing posts and pillars
Decorative hardware

Secondhand but Not Old

Parts of furniture
Radio, record, television cabinets
Bedsteads
Parts of wooden baby cribs (complete ones are now too costly to use for rebuilding)
Benches
Nightstands
Chests
Cupboards
Boxes
Beveled boards
Tables

Where to Look for Old and Secondhand Items:

Read your newspaper ads and check the Yellow Pages of the telephone book for the following.

Auctions
Sales: Garage, estate, stock-thinning, close-out, rummage and charity, antique
Thrift Stores: Goodwill, Salvation Army, St. Vincent dePaul and many others
Secondhand stores
Antique shops
Wrecking yards and salvage stores

NEW

Unfinished chests and cupboards (for specific projects)
Turned legs and spindles
Metal corners and brackets
Casters
Beveled boards and moldings
Shelves

Wooden brackets
Metal hardware
Tools and construction aids (see Catalogs, below)
Reproductions
Handles and knobs
Carved or pressed wood, metal or brass ornaments

This category includes a marvelous array of products made especially for do-it-yourselfers: spindles, knobs, moldings and the like. Visit stores that carry these items occasionally—even if you prefer old things—in order to keep up with current trends in the new products. Some of these items may prove remarkably helpful when it comes to rebuilding.

Where to Look for New Things:

Unfinished furniture and woodworking shops
Do-it-yourself sections of hobby, variety, department and Handyman stores
Lumberyards
Hardware stores

Catalogs to Send For: (This is a partial listing. There are others equally good, and you may receive some of them in the mail too, after requesting catalogs listed here.)

Brookstone Catalog
Hard-to-Find Tools and other fine things
Brookstone Company
127 Vose Farm Road
Peterborough, NH 03458

Constantine's Catalog for Woodworkers
Albert Constantine and Son, Inc.
2050 Eastchester Road
Bronx, NY 10461
(Enclose $.50 for catalog)

Woodworkers Catalog
Creative materials for the creative craftsman
The Woodworkers Store
21801 Industrial Blvd.
Rogers, MN 55374
(Enclose $1.00 for catalog)

Later on, I'll show you just how practical all this collecting can be. But don't confine your thinking to any one period when you look for material. Do consider possibilities from yesterday, today and tomorrow. Then choose what will serve you best from all three.

Part Two

Make-over Magic

4
Doll Beds

There are dozens of inexpensive items you can convert into handsome accessories or turn into gifts that give no hint of what they once were. Nor will anyone know their cost, since they'll be one of a kind.

Doll beds can become a hobby in themselves. For instance, you can build a four-poster that has an ornate headboard and footboard, or a bed having shorter posts; you might prefer a more elaborate canopy or no canopy at all and so on: all sorts of variations are possible.

Diagram 3a shows how a four-poster might be constructed utilizing a table's top and legs. The beds shown in Plates 15 and 16 consist of five basic parts: frame, headboard, posts, feet and canopy. It contains material taken from this same secondhand table. (Diagram 3b.) (Not that I'm recommending all such tables be dismantled and turned into doll beds; some are fairly solid and not bad looking. But others, as tables, are useless, and these you might look upon as potential building material.)

Plate 15: Canopy doll bed by the author is made from a wooden letter tray, baluster posts, and wooden drawer pulls.

Plate 16: The doll bed is finished in natural wood tones. Accessories are blue and white.

There are of course other types of salvage and new products, too, that you can use for assembling a doll bed. For now, though, let's assume you intend building a doll bed similar to the one pictured in Plates 15 and 16. I'll simply explain how I assembled this particular bed, then you can use whatever part of the directions are needed as you move along a step at a time with your own construction.

Directions for Canopy Doll Bed

Framework. A wooden letter tray, 10¼ inches wide by 15 inches long, serves as a ready-made frame for the canopy bed.

Headboard. The lower shelf of the table in Diagram 3 forms the bed's headboard. But whatever type of board you use, it should be no less than ⅝ inch thick (and not plywood—more about this later).

Step 1. Sides of the shelf/headboard are sawed off to the width of the letter tray frame, as shown in Diagram 4a. Round the sawed-off edges of the headboard with a wood rasp, then sand smooth.

Step 2: Join Headboard to Frame. (Remember to start holes always by pounding in the point of a nail before drilling.) Drill two holes in the end of your letter tray frame (I used a 5⁄32-inch bit, and for the two corresponding holes in the headboard, a 1⁄16-inch bit.) To do this, first drill holes in the *frame.* Lay headboard on workbench with curved end of letter tray frame flat against it, keeping bottom and side edges even. Then, with the point of a nail inserted through holes in frame, mark exact location for corresponding holes on the *headboard* before drilling. Don't try to drill straight through the frame and into the headboard unless you have some way of clamping or holding both the frame and board firmly in place while you drill.

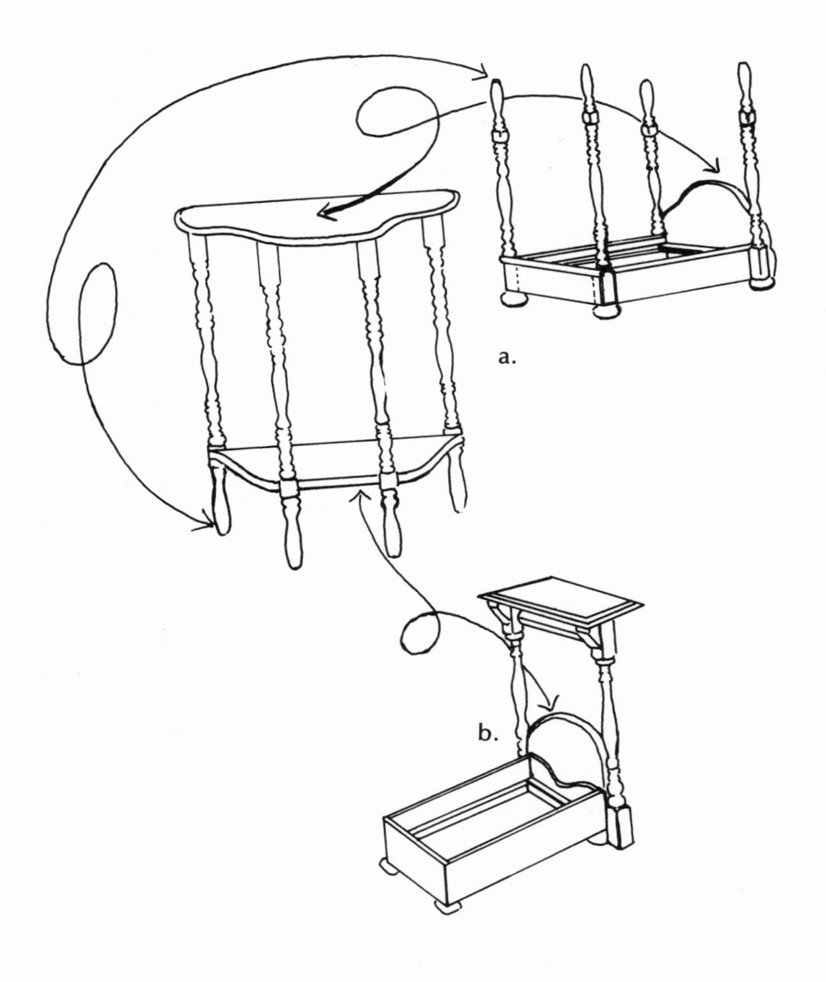

Diagram 3

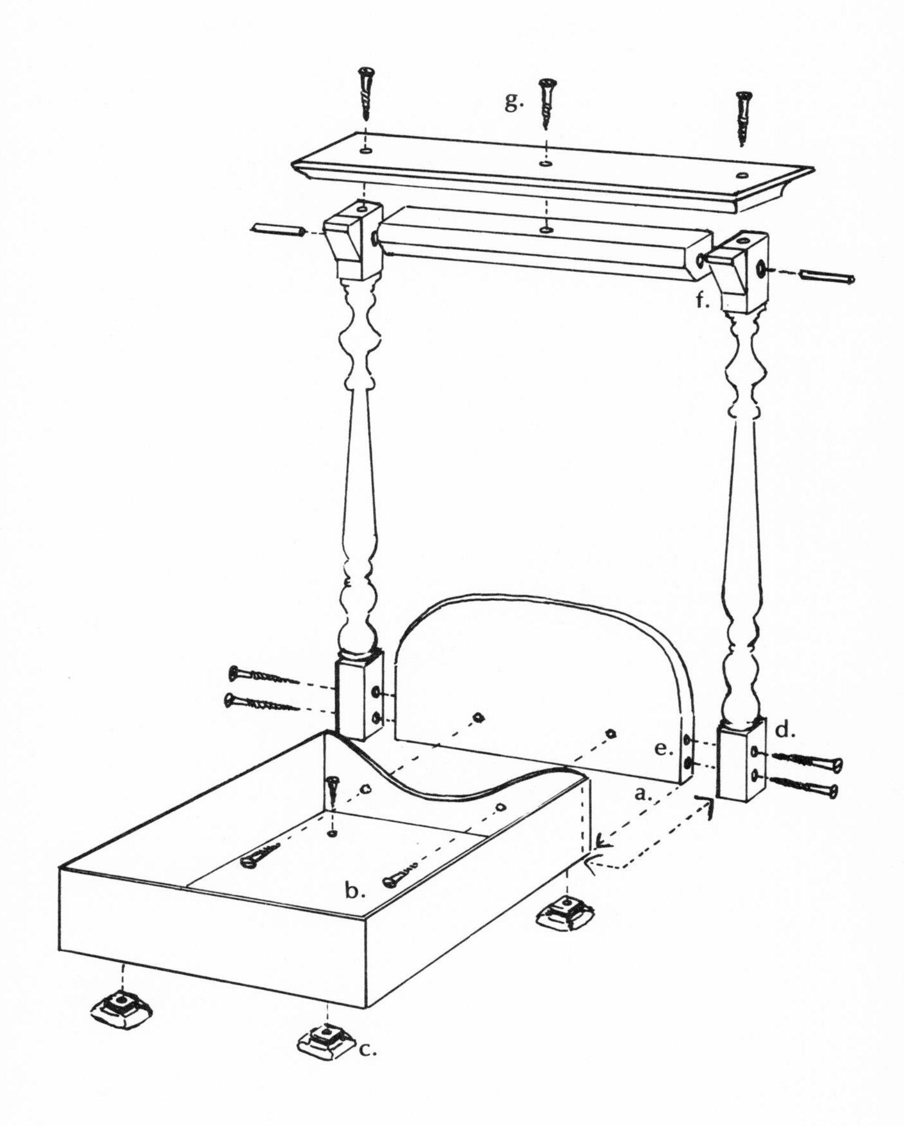

Diagram 4

Step 3. Next, use sandpaper on end of frame and on corresponding portion of headboard before coating with all-purpose glue the areas to be joined. Wait a moment for glue to become tacky, then fasten the frame to the headboard with two screws (Diagram 4b), taking pains to select screws that are short enough so their points will not protrude from the back of the headboard.

Note: As mentioned in Chapter 2 (see instructions for Coatrack), screw heads should be set down into the wood so you can plug or putty over them before staining or painting. However, in joining the frame and headboard, I countersunk the heads of the two screws only enough to make them level with the inside surface of the letter tray frame—since it is constructed of fairly thin wood, and the screw heads might break through if set in too deeply.

Feet. Four new drawer pulls (unfinished wood) are used as feet (Diagram 4c). At this point, stop and consider the style of your bed. Try to visualize how the posts you have chosen, and the feet, will look when the bed is finished, then decide which to add next.

Originally, I connected the posts first to this bed, lining them up with the bottom of the frame. But once the feet were on, the posts appeared suspended in midair. So I took out the screws and reset the posts at floor level—hence the designs on their outer sides, where I glued on bits of decorative molding to conceal the leftover screw holes. Later, I added two more tiny pieces, one at the top of each post, to cover the holes where posts and canopy were joined. Surprisingly, this gave the ornamentation a unified look, as if it were planned that way.

Step 4: Attach the Feet. The drawer pulls used here already have center holes. Mark their location when you position the feet on the bottom of your doll bed, and these can serve as a starting point for drilling holes in corners of the frame. Select screws that will fit in these ready-made drawer-pull holes. (I used four No. 10 screws, 1 inch long.)

Remember, as you position the feet, to be sure the back ones are set far enough in so their bottom edges will not interfere with the posts or hold them out away from the frame. If necessary, you can trim the feet a bit with a knife.

To drill holes in corners of the frame, I used a 13/64-inch bit. When these holes are drilled and you're ready to attach the feet, coat contact areas with glue before you insert and tighten the screws.

Posts. Two small baluster posts were used to support the canopy. Before you begin, square off the ends of your baluster posts if they are angled, but save the cutoff pieces. (See Step 8 and Diagram 5.)

Note: Posts for this project must have a squared section at the top (for attaching to canopy) and a squared segment at the bottom (where the posts are joined to the headboard and frame).

Step 5: Drill Holes and Attach Posts. Line posts up with headboard and mark where the holes will be drilled, as shown in Diagram 4d. Clamp posts in vise, start holes with a nail, then drill clear through posts, two holes in the lower section of each, with an 11/64-inch bit. As indicated on the chart at the end of Chapter 2, a 2-inch No. 8 screw will slip easily into this hole.

However, for the threaded end of the screws which go into the headboard, drill each of the four holes (two on each side) with a smaller, 5/32-inch bit—after using a nail to mark centers. As you can see, this is why your headboard must be at least 5/8 inch thick—so there will be enough room to drill holes in its edges (Diagram 4e)—and why headboard should not be made of plywood: screws don't hold well in the edges of plywood.

While you have your drill out, (since it is easier to drill holes in the posts before they're fastened to the bed) clamp *top* sections of posts in vise one at a time and drill another hole through each, this time using a 13⁄32-inch bit (if your posts are thick enough; if not, select a smaller one). These holes will be used later for joining the posts to the canopy brace.

One more thing: before you fasten lower sections of the posts to your headboard with the 2-inch screws, drill countersink holes for the heads of the screws in the posts. (See directions for Coatrack in Chapter 2.) Later, after the doll bed was done, I added a third screw in each post, by drilling a hole through the rounded lower section and into the edge of the headboard. You may not need this, depending on the contour and thickness of your posts.

Remember to sand, and coat all contact areas with glue before tightening the screws.

Step 6: Selecting a Canopy and Brace. In choosing these, I experimented with cardboard to get the exact measurement and considered a variety of boards for both the canopy and brace to see what would look best.

An unfinished beveled board, 5½ inches by 15 inches (the kind tole painters use) was made into a canopy by turning the board upside down, with the beveled edge underneath and the flat side on top.

The brace that goes lengthwise under the canopy was cut from a long board, 1½ inches by ¼ inch in thickness. However, a plain piece of 1-inch lumber or something of comparable size would do equally well.

Now Attach the Brace. Since you have already drilled a hole in the top section of each post, the next step is to drill a corresponding one in each end of the brace (Diagram

4f). Again, I used a 13⁄32-inch bit. A 3⁄8-inch dowel will fit into this hole with a little room left over so you can adjust the brace level with the tops of the posts.

There are two reasons for using dowels here instead of screws. One, a wooden dowel allows more leeway for adjustment. Two, it eliminates any possibility of running into horizontal screws later when you drill downward into the posts and brace (for attaching the top board).

Note: Ordinarily, the correct way to ensure that a dowel will line up perfectly with the hole it's intended for would be to use a *dowel center* (although I didn't use one here). Sets of these are inexpensive, and may be helpful; you simply insert the correct-sized center in a dowel hole drilled in one of two parts to be joined, then press or tap the two parts together. A point will mark hole center locations precisely on the mating part.

Mix Epoxy and Glue Dowels in Place. Find a spot for your doll bed where it won't be moved for several hours. Then, after dowels have been cut to the proper length (approximately 1¾ inches) and all areas have been sanded, mix epoxy glue with a flexible knife and put into the holes along with the dowels. (Epoxy works best here, since it adds thickness and body. And it won't dry instantly, which means you can take time to line things up—if the brace needs leveling, push a sliver of wood down into one side of the hole, or pack in a bit of paper or foil to even it.)

Apply clamps or weights wherever needed as you go along. (I sometimes detach and use the rubberized clamps from my Christmas floodlights. These are very handy for small gluing jobs.)

Step 7: Fasten Canopy Board to Brace and Posts. Let epoxy set—preferably overnight—then check again to see if brace and tops of posts are level by setting the canopy

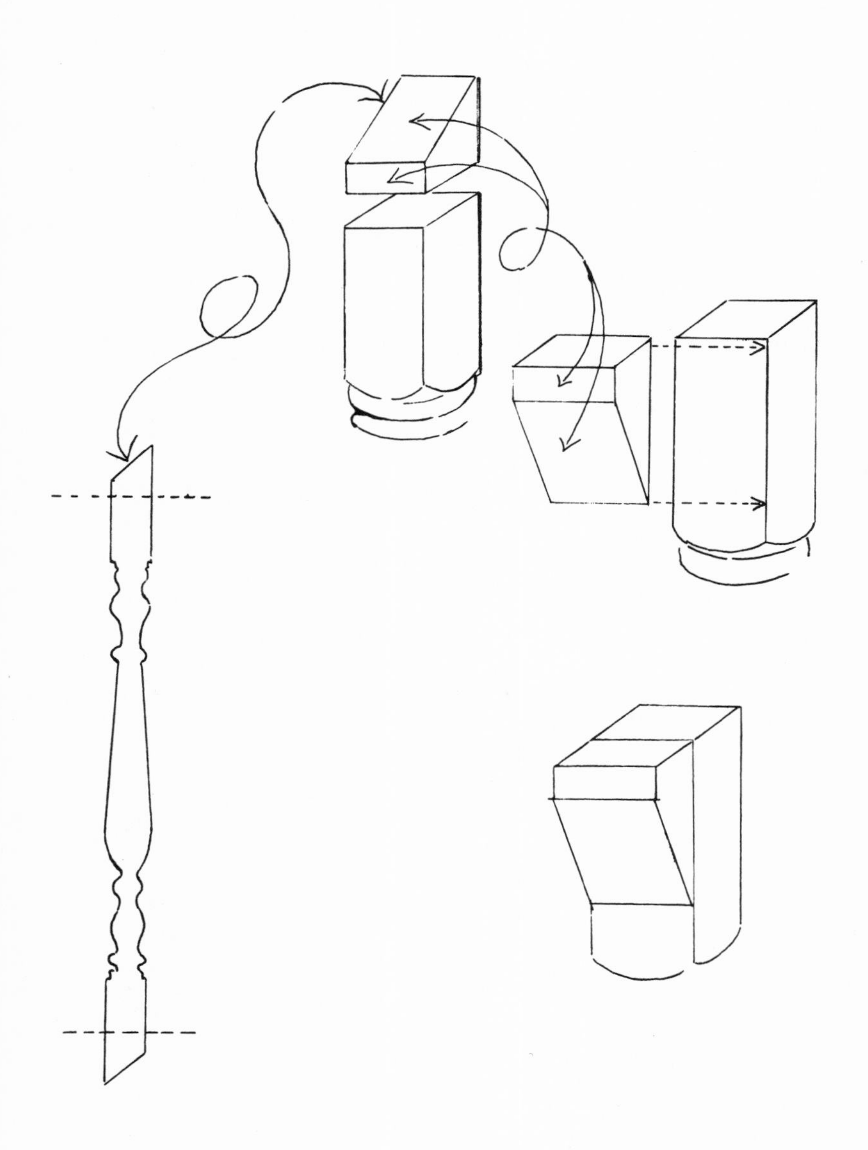

Diagram 5

board on them. If there are high spots, clamp posts and/or brace—one side at a time—in your vise. Smooth top with the wood rasp and sandpaper before you attach the canopy board with three screws as illustrated in Diagram 4g. Remember to first drill holes in the canopy board. Mark corresponding hole locations on brace and posts. Then, with bed held firmly or clamped in vise, drill downward into brace and posts.

Step 8. The angled front braces (sawed-off ends of baluster posts—see Diagram 5) were added mostly for appearance and were glued into place with all-purpose glue.

One thing more, while you have the glue out: Unless the mattress for your bed is going to be quite thick, you'll need to glue strips of wood inside your letter tray frame (Plate 15). This is where the mattress will rest—on a thin board or heavy cardboard cut to fit.

Step 9. Instead of painting this bed, I decided to give it an oil finish; a half-and-half combination of boiled linseed oil and turpentine rubbed in, then wiped off. See Chapter 13. In some places, where wood was very light colored or putty was evident, I added a touch of brown stain (burnt umber).

Step 10: Screw Eyes (to support canopy curtain). One small step and your bed is done—ready for whatever frills you want to add. Turn bed upside down. Make indentations at intervals around the under edge of the canopy board with a small finishing nail, for screw eyes—the kind you use for attaching wire to the back of picture frames—that will support the canopy curtain. Look closely and you'll see them underneath the top board in Plate 15.

Curtain. The curtain is simply a piece of material approximately 40½ inches long, doubled over to keep the wrong side of the material from showing inside the canopy—but with the bottom edges left open and hemmed separately so curtain will hang nicely.

To allow for fullness, the curtain should be wide enough to go at least one and one-half times around the back and both sides of the canopy bed. My curtain measured 42 inches overall, including ½-inch turn-unders for side hems.

Front Canopy Flounce. This is separate, but strung on the same elastic as the curtain. (See Plate 16.) Stitch a casing to run elastic through in top of canopy curtain and in the front flounce (no heading). Use very narrow elastic and gather curtain enough so that when ends of elastic are sewn together it will form a circle (about 8 inches in diameter). Elastic must be snug enough to hold firmly between the underside of the canopy board and the screw eyes. I pried the screw eyes open a bit with a screwdriver after they were in the board so they'd grip the top of the curtain more securely.

Mattress. If foam rubber (1½ to 2 inches thick) is used for the mattress, add a little padding on top for roundness before covering it with the same fabric as the pillows, or with any leftover material. Otherwise, it will look flat, as if the bedspread were laid over a board.

Tiebacks. A doubled band of material (1 inch wide) is stitched to the white eyelet tiebacks on either side and extends across the back of the canopy curtain. This keeps the curtain from billowing out in back. It also anchors the eyelet tiebacks since they are pinned to the band from underneath with tiny safety pins.

The magic of do-it-yourself gives a piece such as this a handcrafted charm not achieved in mass production, possibly because it reflects the joy in *creating*—or the simple enchantment of a gift made with care, thought and love.

5

Personalized Mirrors and Frames

It's great fun to rescue a shabby relic of a frame and turn it into a decorating success. A frame that appears completely hopeless may be worth buying if it's inexpensive.

Framed Bulletin Boards

If you don't want to go to the expense of having a mirror made for an old frame there are other options. For example, a bulletin board can be easily made by inserting plywood-backed cork. The idea for a more complex style, as shown in Plate 17, was sparked by an unexpected flaw in a thrift store frame. Stripping uncovered two badly scorched areas in one corner.

The burns were too deep to sand out. Rather than paint such an interesting frame I covered the charred spots with a slender post and balanced it with a matching one on the opposite side. Not only was the scorched area a surprise, but the frame also turned out to be hardwood—another good reason for not painting it.

Plate 17: Bulletin board by the author utilizes a shelf and posts to recycle a damaged frame.

Again, this is what recycling is about—making the most of features you don't anticipate beforehand in items that you buy. And this includes not only surprise problems but unexpected good points as well.

For example, the corners of the frame were not mitered, but put together with two full-length sidepieces extending the height of the frame. A bonus building tip acquired from studying this frame is the lapped-corner idea which could be adapted to various projects—for instance, to frame the front of a bookcase, or trim a wall piece or a cupboard door.

Construction steps used in assembling the framed bulletin board and shelf are detailed later on in this chapter.

Miscellaneous Frames and Mirrors

Consider all the potentials when buying framed pictures and mirrors or any type of empty frame, because renovation may range all the way from simple refurbishing to reconstruction.

Let's suppose you find a nice little framed mirror that is too small to be of any decorative significance. One way to give it added importance and style is to mount it—frame and all—in the center of three folding panels. Put these together with small brass hinges. The panels may be either painted and antiqued, or given a natural wood finish. Another way to use this type of mirror for maximum effect is described in Chapter 7, under "Oak Wall Planter."

It is possible to restore a mirror that is spotty and clouded and seemingly worthless by having the back resilvered. (This service isn't available in every area.) The one thing that resilvering won't accomplish is to remedy scratches on the glass itself, so check any mirror you intend to buy by running your hands carefully over the surface of the glass to detect any deep scratches. Also, unless a mirror has a beveled edge, it is probably not worth restoring.

The mirror shown in Plate 18 has a plain edge. But when you consider buying this type of piece, do consider both the frame and the mirror, then ask yourself if the price is right.

For instance, this ravaged mirror in the heavily painted frame, complete with corner trim, was only seventy-five cents at a garage sale. The same piece might cost three or four dollars—perhaps more—at a thrift shop simply because it's old. I probably wouldn't have bought it at that price since the unbeveled mirror would not warrant resilvering. Also, the frame, while it appeared to be oak, had been carelessly nailed together at the corners. Add

Plate 18: "Before" photo of old frame.

Plate 19: Frame is shown recycled with wooden brackets and candle cups (salt and pepper shaker tops).

to this the time, work and material for removing the paint, plus the unknown condition of the wood underneath, and you can see it might be a poor bargain.

At a price of seventy-five cents, however, it was worth the effort of stripping to see if the oak underneath might be restorable. And, I hoped to salvage two or three of the brass corner pieces to use as trim on something else. The refurbished frame is shown in Plate 19.

Candleholder Frame

Corners of the frame had been reinforced with large nails. In such old wood, removing them could be a risky process. Because of this, I simply pried the corners apart a bit, squeezed in glue, then gave each corner a few raps with the hammer to tighten it and wiped off excess glue with a damp cloth.

Four wide rubber-band-type clamps (ordered from one of the catalogs mentioned in Chapter 3) were tightly crisscrossed on the frame to hold the corners in place until the glue had dried.

Other flaws were uncovered once the thick coat of dingy white paint had been stripped away. I found there were a few deeply stained, dark areas in each corner. These stains were impossible to remove, so the obvious answer was to cover them as best I could. The two corner pieces (glued on each corner at top of frame) are reproductions of a wooden corner trim that was used on Victorian frames.

These, along with the candleholder brackets, serve not only as ornamentation on the frame, but provide reinforcement, as well.

Candle Cups and Brackets. The candle cups are simply the wooden screw-on tops from a tall pair of wooden salt and pepper shakers. Fortunately, existing holes in these tops (for dispensing salt and pepper) were inconspicuously centered, and I enlarged a center hole in each top (to ⅜ inch) for attaching the cups to the brackets. These holes were drilled with the tops screwed onto their bases so they could be clamped in the vise for drilling. Cups were attached to the brackets with a short length of threaded lamp rod. See Diagram 6c.

Brackets used to support the cups are shown "before" in Diagram 6b. (These would also make excellent shelf brackets.) In adapting them for candleholders I reshaped them a bit. First, a diagonal cut with the saw, then, a notch, rounding the bracket slightly to follow the lines of the grooved design on its side. And finally a touch-up with coarse, then very fine sandpaper.

A second hole (in addition to the existing one) was drilled in each bracket for fastening it to the frame. To mark points on brackets where the candle cups were to go, each bracket was first hung on the wall in the same position it would later assume on the frame. The candle cup was then balanced on the bracket at the proper angle and, through the candle cup's center hole, its exact location marked on the bracket arm. Clamping each bracket in the vise, a hole was drilled in it for attaching the cup, taking pains to see that the bracket remained in an upright position (so hole could be drilled straight down into the bracket arm).

Next, epoxy glue was packed into these holes while each bracket arm was still clamped in the vise in proper position. A 2-inch length of threaded lamp rod was set into the epoxy in each hole and carefully braced (with slivers of wood) to ensure that the rod stayed upright until the epoxy had hardened.

The final step was to slip each candle cup plus a metal washer onto the lamp rod, add a screw-on hexagon nut and tighten, adjusting and leveling the candle cup at the same time. Although not essential from a construction

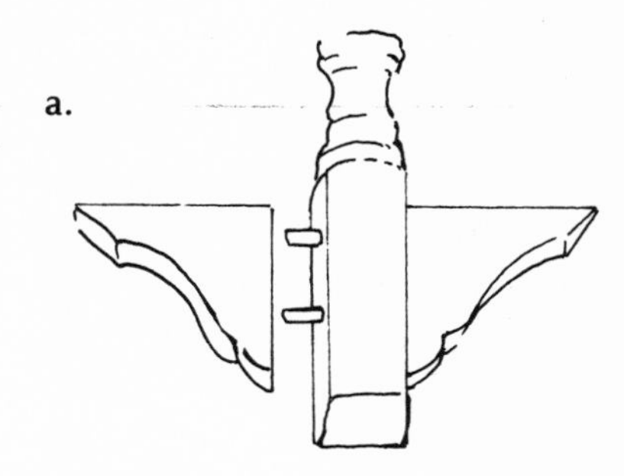

b. Post brackets used for candleholder frame (Plate 19)

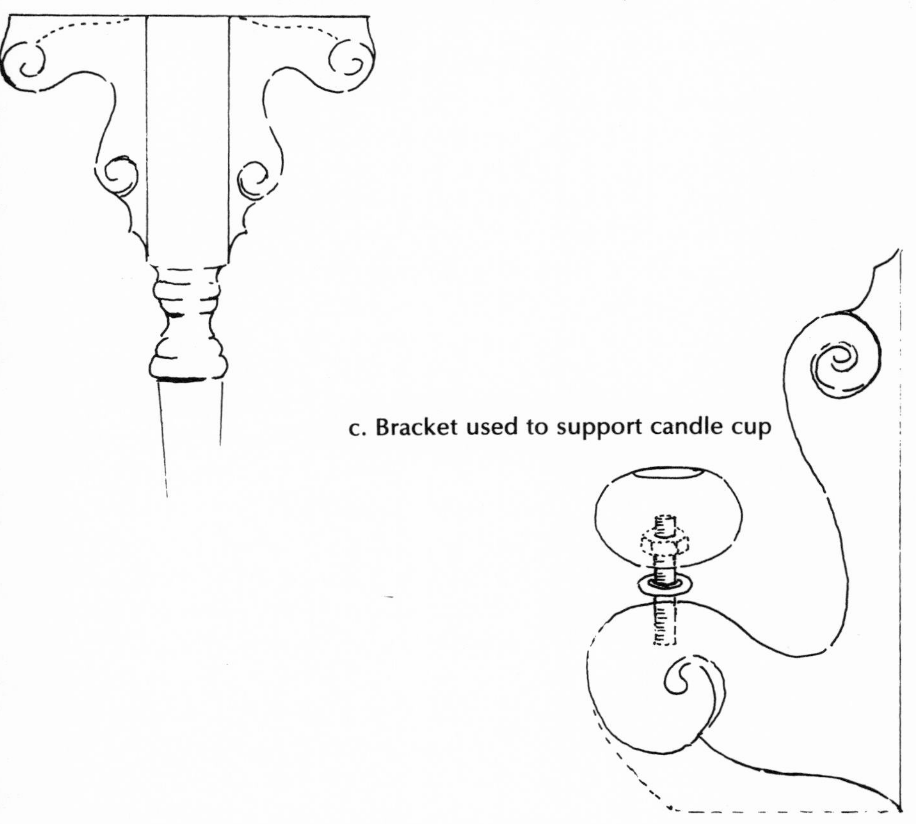

Diagram 6: Small post brackets suitable for shelf supports or wall pieces.

standpoint, I added a small brass seating ring to the lamp rod underneath the candle cup just because it looked nice.

The wood-finishing process for this particular frame was unusual in that the candle cups and corner trim required bleaching in order to match the frame. I've used this piece in detailing this procedure in Chapter 13, under the heading, "How to Make Woods Match."

The bulletin board frame discussed at the beginning of this chapter (and shown in Plate 17) is also a composite, utilizing wood from different sources. Directions for its assembly follow.

Bulletin Board Frame with Shelf

Preliminary Steps. After the frame is stripped (see Chapter 13) and has dried thoroughly, sand it well, paying particular attention to grooves where varnish or paint buildup may remain. Run a pointed knife or ice pick along these grooves to remove any residue.

Follow same procedure with the posts.

Note: It is sometimes almost impossible to get every trace of old varnish out of deep designs or grooves. So when you're refinishing, if shiny or light spots are noticeable, touch them with burnt umber (artists' oil color) on a toothpick or tiny brush and allow to dry overnight or longer before any further finish is added.

Assembling Frame. Square off bottoms of posts by laying them in position on frame and pencil-marking underside of posts along edge of frame. Clamp both posts in vise. Using a square, continue lines down outer sides of posts and saw off along lines.

While posts are still clamped in vise, drill two holes in bottom section of each. (I used a No. 10 three-in-one drill and countersink bit. Consult the chart in Chapter 2 and select a bit consistent with the size of your posts.) These holes must be counterbored to allow room for the wooden buttons.

Lay posts on frame to mark frame for drilling. Mark with point of nail inserted through holes in posts. Drill holes, then fasten each post lightly to frame with one screw before marking top of post where it should be squared off even with the frame.

Preparing Posts for Fastening to Frame. Next, unscrew posts, clamp both in vise and saw off tops.

While posts are in vise, drill one hole in top section of each post for attaching to frame. Repeat procedure used for bottom sections.

Place posts on frame to mark it for drilling top holes. Drill holes in frame. Now oil frame before the posts are attached permanently. (Wipe well, clean grooves with soft rag over a knife point. Then oil posts.)

Note: Woods such as cedar and fir are sometimes rather lifeless with nothing but oil. The addition of a coat of satin-finish varnish imparts just enough luster to make the wood look finished and attractive.

Wooden Hole Plugs. At some upholstery shops you can buy flat-ended wooden plugs and rounded buttons—used here on the posts to conceal screw holes—or order them in a variety of sizes and different woods from a wood products catalog (see list in Chapter 3).

The wooden buttons used for this particular frame, however, were six small knobs from the hardware store. I sawed off each of them with an X-acto knife, then further reduced the diameter of the shank by trimming with a knife as you would sharpen a pencil, so that the knob's cutoff end fit neatly into the screw hole. This *is* doing it the hard way, and I recommend that you acquire some of the ready-made plugs.

Attaching Shelf. The shelf—a narrow board, cut to length, oiled and finished to match frame and posts, was added last. See directions for attaching shelf to wall piece on page 93.

Varnishing. After the necessary holes have been drilled and the screws tested for size, length and so on, and the parts oiled, varnish the posts, frame and shelf separately before permanently assembling them. Ordinarily, this would be done after assembly, but with the posts fastened to the frame, it is difficult to maneuver a brush and do a smooth job of varnishing.

The finished bulletin board, including posts, hole plugs, frame and shelf contains at least three kinds of wood. I first tried staining some areas darker, some lighter (before varnishing) to compensate for the differences in wood. This works well in some cases, but didn't here. The slight variance in color of parts of the assembled frame detracted from the overall design until a light coat of *antiquing* was applied.

Lightly done, this process does not conceal the grain of the wood or take away from the natural effect. (For more on this, see Chapter 13, under "Pull It Together with Antiquing.")

Cork used for the bulletin board is glued (and clamped) at center and along edges to thin plywood backing cut to fit inside the frame. Install this as you would a picture, using tiny brads, or a staple gun.

Spanish Frame

The silver-trimmed Spanish-type frame in Plate 20 is an example of wood combined with metal for dramatic effect.

Silvered upholstery tacks were used to nail down separate links taken from two decorative ladies' metal belts of different designs—one an oxidized aluminum belt with

Plate 20: Frame trimmed with decorative links from two metal belts.

round links, the other made up of oblong-shaped links in some type of metal with a silvery look. However, once the conglomerate pieces were tacked onto the oak frame, they appeared to be truly silver, giving the frame an ancient look like something found in an old Spanish mission. This type of frame did in fact seem particularly suited to the decoration.

Tacks were placed through existing holes where links of the belts were originally joined together by a flat narrow chain.

Note: In order to mellow the appearance of the decorative metal and make it look old, I antiqued the trim *lightly* with a mixture of Payne's grey and ultramarine blue and viridian. (See Chapter 13, under "Antiquing.")

This may not be necessary, and probably wasn't needed here, but I wanted to try it—and found it does work, so for metal that is quite shiny, it's something to remember. If the metal is very slick or highly lacquered, better give it a quick coat of low gloss varnish first and let it dry before antiquing so the antiquing mixture won't just run off.

I had originally intended trimming this frame with brass or gold leaf, but the color of the oak when stripped was a soft grayed color like driftwood or old barn siding, and silver seemed more suited to it.

Problems encountered in refurbishing this frame—once it was stripped—included four places on the face of the frame where holes had been drilled completely through it, then filled with white putty.

I could of course have *painted* the frame to cover the putty-filled holes, but since I wanted to retain the aged look of the wood, the only answer was to camouflage these ugly spots. I think the resulting flawed, knotholed effect is quite acceptable on a primitive-looking frame such as this.

In doing renovation of this sort, where the purpose of the cover-up is to fool the eye, the secret of a skillful paint job is to overlay your work at various stages with a thin coat of dull varnish. The process can be tricky, and if you work on it too long, perhaps you'll undo some of the effect you've achieved. For this reason, when it begins to look right—stop. Let antiquing dry *thoroughly*—a couple of days or more if you've used a lot of oil paint. When dry, put a coat of low gloss varnish over it. Now your artwork is sealed, and if it still needs a bit more paint here and there, you can safely work on it without destroying what you've already accomplished.

Just remember to cover each stage of your artwork (after it has dried) with another thin coat of varnish.

In the end, despite problems I didn't expect, this piece turned out to be a very good buy. Since the mirror itself was basically good, I had it resilvered.

There are dozens of ways you can personalize mirrors and frames, and make them as individual as your signature. Start by collecting pictures of interesting or unusual frames. Visit antique stores; some of these shops can be a real source of inspiration, where you may find pieces of decorative brass or wood trim that you can adapt as ornamentation.

6

Wall Pieces

For wall pieces, there is a formula of sorts. The basic ingredients are boards of various kinds and shapes, and/or frames. These are used to form a background for additional components—brackets, shelves, mirrors, small drawers, coat hooks, moldings and ornamental wood or metal trim.

Obviously, this is a marvelous way to utilize pretty hardwood parts and pieces from old furniture, particularly the smaller odds and ends and leftovers—beautiful bits of nothing such as ornate moldings or carved trim, or beveled boards that might, in a moment of housecleaning fervor, be destroyed and gone forever simply because one doesn't quite know what to do with them, or grows tired of moving them around.

Note: Often you'll collect nearly enough parts for a project, then have to wait until just the right thing comes along. Perhaps a pair of brackets is needed and some

Plate 21: Shadow box frame by the author is made from a recycled chair seat.

fancy trim, a mirror or a nice backboard. That's why it's important to plan your wall piece first by trying all sorts of things. Lay the pieces out together, and study them for size and design until you hit on a pleasing combination.

Painted Wall Piece

As I mentioned in Chapter 1, the decorative wall shelf (Plate 1) was assembled from an assortment of wooden odds and ends left over from various periods. The woman who built the wall piece started with a shelf board that was nicely beveled on three sides and had antique trim suspended underneath the front edge. Since it would have been a pity to cut off so handsome a relic, she selected a backboard that could be trimmed to the width of the shelf.

After centering the ornamental top (possibly part of a mirror frame) on the backboard, the ends were sawed off to fit. Assembly of the wall piece was done with screws and glue in the following order:

1. Ornamental top attached to backboard
2. Shelf fastened to backboard (see directions for attaching shelf to shadow-box wall piece, in this chapter). The shelf was first trimmed by ½ inch along the back edge (so it would be the same depth as the brackets plus the grooved sidepieces)
3. Sidepieces fastened to backboard
4. Brackets screwed to backboard from behind, and from underneath, to shelf
5. Curtain rod finials added to brackets
6. Small bits of ornamental wood glued to sidepieces (to cover heads of screws, and joining cracks)

The entire wall piece was painted Spanish gold, then antiqued with burnt and raw umber.

Shadow Box Wall Piece

Preparing Components for Assembly. When you consider the wide range of sizes, shapes and materials that could be used for, say, just a backboard, it is apparent that no two wall pieces need be alike. An oak chair seat forms a backboard for the finished shadow box in Plate 21. I first removed the broken caning, then turned the chair seat over, using the underside of it for my backboard/frame since there was a groove cut in the top for the caning. The underside of the seat was a bit rough and needed sanding with an electric sander.

Except for areas to be glued (see below, "Preliminary Step: Wooden Ornament,") I oiled—and stained wherever necessary—the separate parts as I went along in order to keep the pieces as nearly the same tone as possible. (Old oak varies as to color; see Chapter 13, under "How to Make Woods Match.")

Brackets. The two leftover ends from the coatrack shelf described in Chapter 2 serve as brackets for this wall piece.*

Shelf. The shelf is a broken chair seat's front section, see Chapter 9, under "Chairs (Seats, Backs, Legs)," complete with the shaped piece of wood that originally formed its decorative front apron. Of course this seat also had a groove where the caning had been inserted. Instead of trying to fill the groove in, I sawed the oak chair front off at this point, which gave me a shelf a little over 3 inches wide—an adequate width for displaying small items.

All of the shadow box components—brackets, shelf, chair-seat/frame and the wooden ornament—were stripped before assembling.† It is worth taking some pains to remove all traces of old varnish since it is impossible to achieve a good oil finish with varnish remaining on the surface.

Preliminary Step: Wooden Ornament. Attach ornament to top of chair-seat/frame before assembling any of the parts. Sand back of wooden ornament before gluing, as well as area at top of frame where it is to go. Apply thin

---

*More about brackets in Chapter 9, under "Odds and Ends of Salvage."

†See Chapter 13 for information on stripping carved or pressed-wood ornament.

coat of glue to both surfaces. Tack ornament in place with four very small brads, using the original nail holes if possible. Clamp in vise between two boards until glue is dry to avoid warping.

Preparation for Attaching Shelf. Lay frame flat on table with back edge of shelf lined up on it about 2 inches from the bottom of the frame. Mark along shelf top and bottom with a pencil (two lines to indicate thickness of shelf). Drill three screw holes in frame, one on each side and one in the middle, staying within the two pencil lines. Drill smaller corresponding holes in the shelf edge for threaded end of screws.

Fastening Shelf to Frame. When you fasten the shelf to the oak frame (from the back) with three screws, don't tighten one screw completely, then the others. Instead, alternate in tightening the three, so that all remain at approximately the same depth. Otherwise, as you tighten a screw at one end, your shelf may dip or tilt in that direction. Tighten screws *temporarily* so you can test the fit of the shelf.

Shaping Brackets. If all the angles in old furniture parts (your prefabricated material) were accurate and precise, you'd simply make every cut using a square, but in working with old wood, you may find variations—a slight warp, one side a bit higher or lower. For this reason, when fitting brackets, mark, trim and sand each one individually (unless you make a groove and set the bracket into it). I usually cut a thin cardboard pattern to get the exact angle before final shaping.

Fitting brackets can be tricky, but this is one place where patience and perseverance can take the place of expertise. Don't be discouraged if a bracket doesn't fit immediately into the angle formed by backboard and shelf. Take it slow and easy. Work with file and sandpaper a step at a time to eliminate high spots.

Note: Occasionally, an old piece of hardwood will be especially hard and resistant to filing with a light-weight wood rasp. For careful shaping use a flat file of heavier metal that is made for filing wood.

To Attach Brackets. An existing hole in the frame happened to be in the right place for *one* of the bracket screws. Marking the location through the hole onto the bracket's back edge, I drilled a corresponding hole (a smaller one for the threaded end of the screw) to attach the bracket.

This helped in lining up the brackets with the frame's edge and marking where they were to go. However, it's usually more satisfactory to glue and clamp brackets in place first, to achieve a closer fit. Then, after the glue has dried, holes can be drilled straight through from the back of the frame and on into the bracket, (using the right bit for thread point of screw) and enlarging the back-of-the-frame hole afterward to countersink the screw head.

For easier assembly, you can attach all components—tightening the screws to see how everything fits together. Then remove them for any adjusting that is needed (noting where each one belongs). It's a little like fitting a garment—you make an alteration here or a change there, before the final assembly.

As for finishing, check the overall color too; if there's a part that needs more stain to make it blend in better, add it now before you varnish. More about this in Chapter 13.

Wooden Plugs. Existing holes in the oak frame were enlarged with a countersink bit to accommodate ready-made ¾-inch wooden buttons. Since these were made of new wood, I stained them with burnt umber oil color mixed with turpentine before gluing them into the holes.

Although these plugs are sold unfinished, they're available in different kinds of wood. You can order them from a catalog; see list in Chapter 3. It's a good idea to order a variety so you can match them to many projects.

Or, the same catalogs and shops that offer these plugs often also sell sets of plug-cutter bits for your electric drill. With these you can cut your own plugs from leftover scraps of the same salvaged board you've counterbored to receive them. This makes matching the wood that much easier.

To Fasten Framed Picture in Place. The already framed photograph happened to fit exactly inside the oak chair-seat/frame—that's what triggered my idea of making a shadow box. To hold the picture in place, I first attached two blocks of wood to the back of the outer frame—one at the top and one at the bottom—snug against the inner frame, then selected a couple of metal parts from my box of odd-lot hardware for securing the inner frame to the wood blocks. This meant that the framed photograph could be easily removed if I wanted to change pictures or substitute a mirror later on.

One point to remember: in fastening wooden blocks to the back of frame, be careful not to drill through to the front side of the frame. Mark a line on your drill bit with tape or even red nail polish so you'll know how deep to go.

Note: Collect odd pieces of hardware from your disassembled furniture, old frames, etc. Sometimes these unlikely bits of metal may be just what you need, say, as a hanger on the back of a wall piece, a brace for connecting two pieces of wood, or even as decorative trim.

Wall Piece Made from Odds and Ends

Sometimes an unpromising purchase works out surprisingly well. The bottom shelf on the wall piece in Plate 5 was a ready-made one I picked up for next to nothing at a porch sale. It had evidently been built for a corner, so it was off center, extending 2 inches longer beyond the bracket at one end than at the other (Diagram 7a).

After trying it right side up on several wall pieces with little success, I turned it upside down on the frame used as backing for this wall piece. The shelf's brackets fit perfectly along the face of the frame. After I sawed off the shelf's ends to the width of the frame, it appeared to have been made to order.

Note: In sawing off a shelf with existing brackets, lay back edge of shelf in position on frame and mark underside of shelf where it intersects with sides of frame.

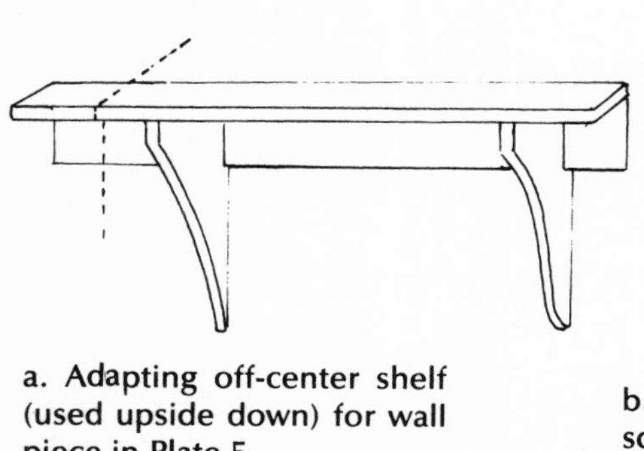

a. Adapting off-center shelf (used upside down) for wall piece in Plate 5

b. Using an odd-shaped scrap of wood to cut a rounded front shelf (Plate 5)

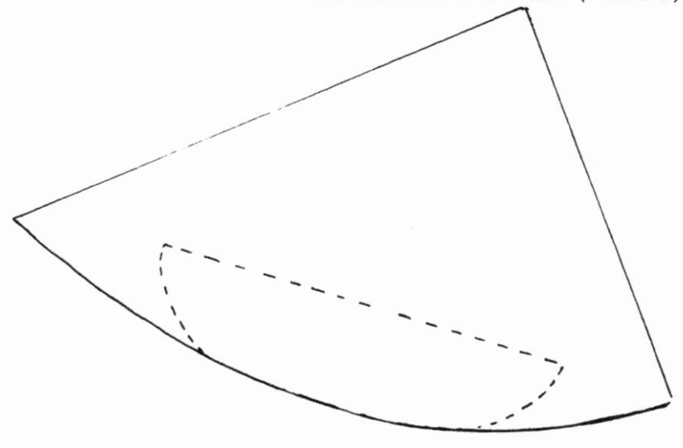

Diagram 7

Use a square to extend each penciled line across the entire end of shelf. Double-check by measuring from each end to bracket to see that the sides are even.

Using the preconstructed shelf saved considerable work, and I changed nothing about it with the exception of removing two screws that fastened the shelf to the brackets (so I could enlarge the drilled holes for countersinking the screws).

As for the frame, it was a solid one but made of coarse-grained lumber—plywood in fact—with a narrow molding that covered all exposed edges. To fill in the open frame, I cut a piece of thin, grooved paneling.

In addition to the preconstructed shelf and the frame and paneling, other components for this wall piece are two narrow decorative boards and a couple of slender 12-inch sections from a pair of turned chair legs plus a top shelf cut from a salvaged board. (Directions for rounded shelves follow.)

To Make a Shelf with a Rounded Front. There are several ways you can do this:

1. Follow directions for cutting the curves for the coatrack board in Chapter 2. (Angle the saw cuts to achieve a curve, then smooth curve with a wood rasp.)
2. Cut shelf from a rounded carving board made for roast meats or turkey. See Chapter 9, under "To Saw Thick Boards or Blocks of Hardwood."
3. Make a rounded shelf from a salvaged board (Diagram 7b). Cut a shelf with rounded front from an odd-shaped, curved-edge board as follows:

Cut a paper pattern for the approximate-size shelf you need, using the board's rounded edge as a partial guide. Fold pattern in half and place it so that the center fold intersects the curve of the board in such a way as to utilize the best portion of the curve. Double-check pattern to be sure it follows curve when opened so both ends of shelf will be the same. Trace pattern onto board. Clamp board in vise and saw along side and back lines. Use wood rasp to blend edges, and sand well.

Use this method for pieces to be painted only, as the grain of the wood may run somewhat on an angle. As I said, the top shelf of this wall piece (Plate 5) is cut from this type of board. The wood is oak, but even so, it looks better painted since the grain runs on the bias, so to speak.

Wooden Trim. The ornamentation at the top of the wall piece was an afterthought. The rounded wooden crown, attached to the frame with two screws, is made by gluing spindle knobs into holes drilled along the outside edge of a piece of wood salvaged from a secondhand chair's wagon-wheel trim.

Other furniture parts of similar shape can be adapted in similar fashion. If no spindles are available, small *new* knobs (from hobby or hardware stores) can be implanted with dowel screws or short lengths of wooden doweling.

Occasionally it's fun to do a stark white piece. This one is sprayed with several light coats of flat white spray paint, sanded, then sprayed again. Stark white is a nice touch for summer or Christmastime decorating. And the white paint can serve as a base coat later if the piece is done over in color and antiqued.

Wall Plaques

The wall plaque in Plate 22 combines three garage-sale items: a board, a pressed-wood ornament and a small recipe file.

The rooster ornament originally had an open, oval frame around it, which was carefully sawed off. The rooster was then painted burnt orange and antiqued. The board and recipe file were stained a deep brown.

Plate 22: Kitchen wall plaque by Betty Breitbarth is painted and antiqued.

Plate 23: Wall piece with dried arrangement by Betty Breitbarth is finished in shades of tan and brown.

After gluing the rooster to the board, the recipe holder was attached with two screws.

Plate 23 shows a plaque assembled from a garage sale board and an old half-circle aluminum pan (originally used for cooking two separate foods on one burner). Two holes were drilled in the pan's flat side for attaching it to the board.

The pan was painted dark brown and the board stained to match. Both were antiqued and coated with satin-finish varnish. The entire arrangement, which includes glazed artificial flowers, teasels and wheat, was done in natural tones of brown and tan.

Whatever your taste in wall pieces—be it an accessory to brighten a wall, or a shelf to display your treasures—there are plenty of secondhand surprises to provide the material you need.

7

Creative Planters

Living plants displayed in lovely containers are a plus factor in any decor. If you've ever priced planters and plant stands in the stores, or wanted to make your own, this could be for you.

Since we've just been talking about wall pieces, let's first consider a wall planter. The components are similar to those you'd use for a wall piece, with the addition of such things as:

1. Half-round containers and nicely shaped cooking pots
2. Ornamental hardware and chains
3. Wooden bowls
4. Brass or copper containers

The shadow box wall piece described in Chapter 6 could easily be converted to a planter by attaching a box of some sort to the frame in place of the shelf.

Plate 24: "Before" photo of old sewing machine cabinet.

Oak Wall Planter

Preliminary Steps. One side of the damaged sewing machine cabinet in Plate 24 serves as a starting point for a wall planter. When this cabinet was disassembled (see Chapter 9) it had already started to fall apart, so I first sanded, then reglued the pieces that made up the side section, putting wide rubber-band clamps around both ways until the glue had dried.*

Next, all tenons—where the side had been joined to the bottom of the cabinet—were sawed off. The result was a

---

*Clamps ordered from Brookstone catalog. (For catalog list, see Chapter 3.)

Plate 25: Oak wall planter with brass towel bar, designed by the author and assembled from old furniture parts.

sturdy paneled oak backboard for the planter which is shown in Plate 25.

A rather ugly piece of oak, shown in Diagram 8a, which had probably been some type of support or frame, was also knocked apart (see Chapter 9) to produce side brackets and a front for the planter box.

The fancy top, or crown, on this piece is a decorative board, with a few added curves done with a friend's router.

Note: A short length of leftover oak flooring was glued edge to edge with the bottom of the board to give it more depth. Combining a couple of narrow boards in this manner is a good way to recycle any board that is narrower than you want it to be.

In fact the one used for the front of the planter box could have been widened in the same way, to improve the overall design and add depth to the box.

To Assemble the Planter Box. Glue brackets in place on backboard, and let dry. Drill screw holes for brackets through backboard from behind and into the edge of the bracket.

The front board on the boxlike plant container overlaps the brackets by about 1 inch. Holes for screws are drilled on each side of this board where it lies on the brackets. (Holes are counterbored so screw heads can be covered with wooden plugs. Mark the location of holes on bracket edges and drill with smaller bit.) Also clamp both brackets in vise and drill a ½-inch hole through rounder lower extensions for the towel bar—a leftover piece of brass pipe from a floor lamp, capped at each end with a curtain rod finial glued into place with epoxy glue. The towel bar can be assembled after wall piece is completed.

Next, cut a paper pattern for bottom of planter box

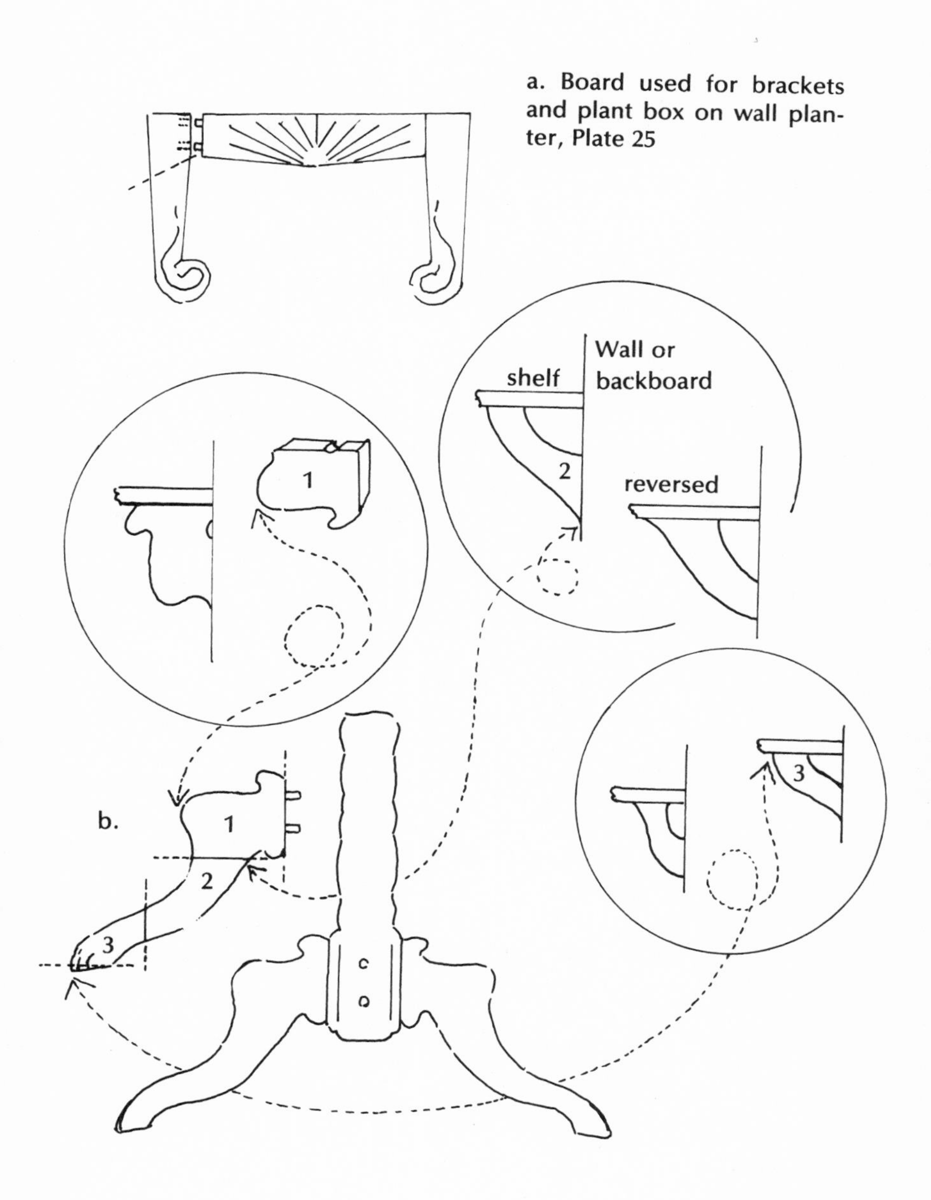
a. Board used for brackets and plant box on wall planter, Plate 25
Wall or backboard
shelf
1
2
reversed
3
b.
1
2
3

Diagram 8

and, using the pattern, cut a thin board to fit *inside* the box. Glue small strips of wood to inner side of brackets to support the box bottom.

Top Shelf. Cut narrow shelf for top of backboard, round corners with rasp and sandpaper. Or adapt a beveled board as was done here. Attach with two screws, using same procedure as for shelf on shadow box wall piece, Chapter 6. Fasten a small bracket underneath each end of shelf with glue and/or screws. See Chapter 9, under "Brackets."

Mirror. A mirror salvaged from a castoff was reframed (at a do-it-yourself frame shop) with narrow molding. Two holes were drilled in each corner of the frame so it could be screwed to the backboard with small brass screws.

In assembling a wall planter, as with previous projects, try fitting pieces together first. Of course you won't use exactly the same material as has gone into this one, but the design can be varied in many ways, yet the same construction methods applied.

For instance, the brass rod was added here because the shape of the brackets suggested it: a preconstructed box or drawer could be substituted for the entire planter-box assembly, thus eliminating the need for a rod; a print or picture might take the place of the mirror and so on.

To visualize changes in a design, try to break a project down into separate parts. Take each component, one at a time, and ask yourself, *What could I substitute for this single piece that would be of similar shape or size and serve approximately the same purpose?* In searching out material for a project, think about doing it in some other medium too. Transpose the piece in your mind's eye from wood into metal, from metal into wood, or whatever.

Naturally, this idea of using alternative materials holds true for the very tall plant stand in Plate 26. There aren't

Plate 26: Components for this tall plant stand by the author are a wooden tray and bowls, an oak tripod and a brass rod.

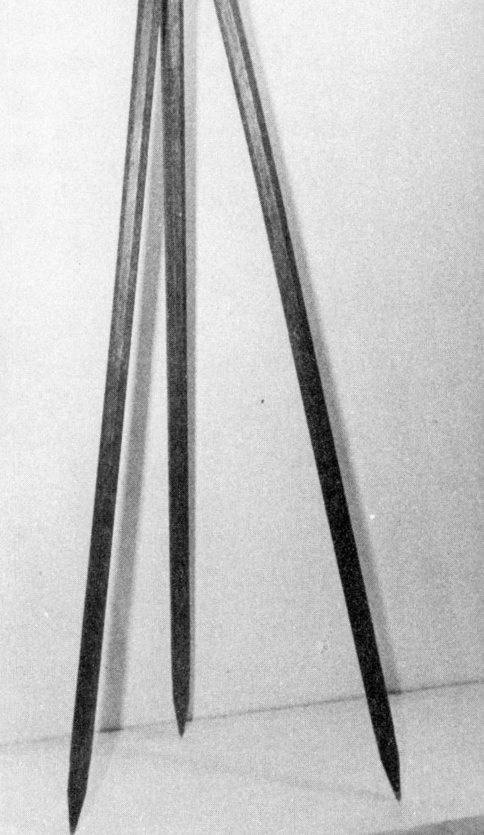

Plate 27: "Before" photo of tripod.

unlimited numbers of oak tripods available. However, since some of these old transit stands had a special-size thread which doesn't fit present-day instruments, and because many of the *old* instruments have worn out or disappeared, you may yet happen onto one of these leftover stands.

Actually, the wooden tripod was itself a substitute for what I'd hoped to find as material. What triggered my idea in the beginning was a picture of an antique plant stand—elegant, 6 feet tall and made of ornate cast-iron rods. Not only that, the stand in the picture wasn't pyramidal in shape; the rods did not converge at the top, but were equidistant around the three identical, evenly spaced ironwork shelves.

Now a wooden tripod (Plate 27) is a far cry from fancy iron, but when you're looking for material to build a specific piece you consider all sorts of things, and apparently my mind was preoccupied with *tall*. The wooden stand too is attractive in its way, although it is totally different from the one I set out to build. You, on the other hand, may go hunting for a tripod but run across some beautiful cast iron instead. And that's the name of the game.

Tall Plant Stand

Preliminary Steps. First, the tripod was stripped with TSP to remove any lingering traces of varnish (see Chapter 13), then sanded well and oiled. Wood tones of the tripod itself were varied—shading from light to dark—so no attempt was made to match tones or shading of other wooden components assembled for the plant stand.

The wooden bowls used here as plant shelves were stripped and oiled, with the exception of the varnished myrtlewood top. Although each of the bowls is a different kind of wood, the contrast is not overly apparent and, for this type of piece, is perhaps more interesting than perfectly matched woods. Also a stand of this height calls for a large trailing plant which tends to create flattering highlights and shadows and further modifies any variance of shading in the wood.

Legs on this type of transit stand are unique; pointed at the base and capped with metal. Rather than saw these points off so the legs could be fastened to the base with screws, I left the ends just as they were and set their metal tips into predrilled holes (see below, "Base"). The original brass fittings of the tripod which had tarnished badly were cleaned and polished with a steel wool pad and a cream polish (available in sporting goods stores and used for polishing spinners).

Other small touches of trim on the finished plant stand include a decorative brass part (shaped like a jar lid) that was adapted for attaching the top and the round head brass screws that were used in assembling the plant stand.

Note: Black metal trim or hardware is as effective.

Base. The base used here consists of a wooden tray with rolled edge glued to a circular piece of oak. Three shallow, evenly spaced holes are drilled in the perimeter of the base. (Mark around base, cut a paper pattern and divide into thirds to establish locations for holes.)

The composite base is attached to the transit stand by drilling a ⅜-inch hole in both the base and the lower bowl/shelf—before it is fastened in place. Then, after shelf is attached to tripod with screws, join bowl/shelf to the base with threaded lamp rod (concealed inside brass tubing). Secure at each end with a metal washer and a hexagon nut. (Or see below, *Note.*)

Tubing is cut with a hacksaw the exact length to fit between the composite base and bottom of wooden bowl, while the lamp rod must be cut a trifle longer to extend inside the bowl and down through center hole in the base.

(The metal washer and nut are then recessed in the underside of the base.)

Note: For easier construction, the base can be done away with altogether; this will also eliminate the need for lamp rod, tubing, etc. But do set metal tips of tripod temporarily into equally spaced holes—drilled in a board or in a piece of plywood—to maintain position of legs during assembly.

As a further aid to construction, the outside circle of decorative brass (found covered with many coats of paint at a thrift store) is slipped down over the tripod from the top to fit snugly around the legs. Alternatives for this might include a circlet of chain, a black wrought-iron loop or a metal belt of some kind.

This serves to further stabilize the legs with their pointed tips set into the base and keeps them in position while the bowl/shelves are wedged into place for measuring and marking locations of screw holes. The metal circlet can either be removed once the stand is assembled or retained as decoration.

Plant Container/Shelf. A wooden nut bowl serves as the lower shelf or plant container. To attach, set tripod on a low table so bowl will be at eye level. Place tips of tripod legs in equidistant hole in base. Brace legs by tying in position or securing with a metal hoop or band. (See instructions above.)

Now position bowl inside tripod at a point where legs are in contact with it and bowl is wedged firmly in place. Adjust and level the bowl, measure to double-check, but trust your eye—be sure it *looks* level too, since the bowl could vary a bit in thickness on one side or the other.

Mark location of bowl on legs and pinpoint locations for screw holes.

Repeat measuring process with smaller bowl. Remove bowls, drill holes through each tripod leg and reposition the bowls inside the tripod to mark them for drilling.

Attach with round head brass screws.

Top of Planter. Any large bowl that looks good can serve as a top. The one used here is flat—more like a tray—and is connected to a lazy Susan base. This works out nicely since the plant can be turned around for sun or watering.

The tripod is ideally constructed for attaching a top to because the metal mounting plate has a center opening big enough for a long screw or bolt. You can use the screw or bolt to attach the lazy Susan base directly—adding a metal washer first. If you haven't a lazy Susan, adapt a wooden bowl, a tray or whatever you choose to serve as a top.

Low Planter on Metal Legs

The planter in Plate 28 is contrived from three totally unrelated pieces. An old stripped-down gas hot plate forms a base for the plant box—a long, narrow drawer placed *lengthwise* on the footed plate. The hot plate required a thorough soaking in an ammonia solution plus scrubbing with a wire brush and steel wool to remove grease and traces of rust before it could be spray painted.

Note: Neither high gloss enamel nor flat black paint will look exactly right on cast iron, so if *wrought-iron-black* paint is not available, spray with flat black, then cover with coat of satin-finish varnish.

The third component, a decorative beveled drawer front (from a different drawer and another era), is attached to the narrow drawer's *side*, giving the planter a carved, made-to-order look.

Plant Box. The front of the plant-box/drawer, which is

Plate 28: Planter by the author is made from a drawer set on a refurbished three-burner gas hot plate.

placed at one end of the hot plate, is chiseled out along the bottom edge so it rests on the metal plate at the same level as the back end (drawer *fronts* are deeper). To do this, make saw cuts at intervals along bottom of drawer front, then use a hammer and chisel to remove wood between the cuts.

To ensure a good fit of wood against metal, bottom edges of the drawer are also chiseled out lightly where corners of hot plate are curved. And one more bit of reconstruction: since the back end of the drawer is made of thinner wood than the front, a second thin board is glued and tacked to the drawer back so that both ends of the plant box will be approximately the same thickness.

To make the planter look finished, attach the pretty drawer front, or any ornamental board of proper size, to the drawer's side, using decorative black hardware, or countersink screws and cover with wooden plugs.

Joining the cast-iron base to the box is optional—I didn't in this case since the drawer's extended side boards effectively locked it into place against an outer ledge of the hot plate, with the recessed bottom of the drawer resting securely on the burner tops.

Set a pan inside the plant box—to hold potted plants and at the same time to protect the box against moisture.

Note: If a gas hot plate is in good condition, you might want to have the legs brass plated and to add matching trim.

Construction details used for this planter will apply to many types of salvage. For instance, instead of old parts and pieces, try using cut-down wooden legs (or even new ones) on a plain box enhanced with present-day synthetic trim, then paint and antique the entire piece.

Plant Stand with Pedestal Base

The stand in Plate 29 utilizes a concave wooden tray as a plant holder—it is fastened to the center post with screws from inside the top of the tray. A ready-made base from an old desk chair, shown "before" in Plate 30, is attached through a center opening in the original chair-base mechanism, to a central pedestal, adapted from an old table leg.

To Assemble Stand. Clamp table leg in vise. Drill a 7⁄16-inch (lamp-rod-sized) hole to a depth of 2 inches in the table leg's lower end. The hole is then filled with epoxy glue,

Plate 29: A table leg, tray and desk chair base form this plant stand by the author.

Plate 30: "Before" photo of old desk chair bases.

and a 6- to 8-inch length of threaded lamp rod inserted while leg is still in vise.* Take care to keep lamp rod from tipping to one side or the other by bracing with wood slivers or foil. The rod must remain perpendicular until epoxy sets. When epoxy has hardened, slip the base onto the rod, add a metal washer, a nut, and tighten.

A touch of ornamental trim is added at the bottom of the table leg where it joins the base—four small metal

*For additional details on this type of construction, see earlier book by this author, *How to Make Something from Nothing*, published by Coward-McCann, Inc., 1968.

decorations, sprayed black and fastened to the leg with tiny screws. This ties in nicely with the black iron on the base which was part of the original desk chair assembly.

Note: Most desk chair bases are put together with cast iron in similar fashion. If there are one or two projections of metal protruding from the top of the base, the table leg can be notched out, or a hole drilled if necessary to accommodate these. Use a chisel or X-acto knife on bottom of table leg until high and low spots are made to correspond with similar uneven areas in the metal. The projections can of course be sawed off with a hacksaw instead, but they do serve a purpose since they hold the table leg stationary and eliminate any possibility of it turning on the base.

The major portion of the stand is its pedestal base which is adaptable for several other projects as well. The addition of a tilted top to the base turns it into a dictionary/reference-book stand. Or, by adding a flat top with a larger surface and a stair-stepped second level containing pigeonholes or drawers, you have a small desk. We'll pursue this subject in the next chapter.
Meanwhile, when it comes to *plant stands*, these may be low, high, or in between, and they afford excellent opportunities to utilize odd-size bases, legs and posts for pedestal construction. Not only that, but various heights of plant holders grouped together make few plants look like many. Remember, plants are a decorator's magic; they can mask an unused chimney, hide an ugly view, or add color, life and style to an otherwise commonplace room.

8

Mix and Match—to Build a Desk

A friend of mine who recently moved from a two-story house into a mobile home, found that much of her furniture was too large to look good in her present low-ceilinged living area. To minimize the investment that all-new furniture would require, she began to look for scaled-down, remodeled furniture and, in the process, came across some clever furniture adaptations.

Small Pedestal Desk

One of my favorites is the compact little desk designed by Mrs. Bernice Fields and mentioned in this book's first chapter. (It is pictured in Plate 4.) This desk was constructed utilizing parts of a secondhand table for the top, four base supports salvaged from a second broken table and, from another, the leg that was used to form the centeral pedestal.

To Attach Base Supports. The four curved extensions that make up the base are doweled into the square section at the bottom of the central leg. Two wooden dowels are implanted in each extension, and corresponding holes are drilled for them in the table leg. (Follow directions for doweling in Chapter 4, but here, use an all-purpose or a wood glue instead of epoxy.)

To Join Base and Pedestal. A wooden plate cut from ¾-inch plywood (and about 8 inches square) is used for fasteneing the desk top to the assembled base. Two screw holes are drilled near the center for joining it to the top of the table leg—and four more holes, one in each corner, for attaching the plate to the desk top with screws from underneath.

Desk Top. The desk top itself consists of the undamaged portion—approximately two-thirds—of a small tabletop. Usable parts of the remaining third are used as trim and to form a narrow shelf. These pieces help to unify the design by repeating the desk top's ornamental molding and beveled front edge.

The shelf is supported by two side brackets salvaged from another source, plus the remains of a broken desk divider, cut down to fit and renailed with tiny brads before being glued into place.

Mix and Match

A desk lends itself particularly well to the use of preassembled parts salvaged from various kinds and periods of furniture. Creative possibilities abound once you visualize the infinite variety of designs that can result simply when legs, bases and tops are *interchanged.* Recycling may mean combining a refurbished tabletop with leftover legs, adding attractive trim to accent a plain desk or applying paint and antiquing to one with a battered finish.

You can create as unique and enchanting a desk as your heart could wish by making the most of salvaged furniture parts and using innovative brackets, shelves, brass trim, ornamental hardware or whatever your imagination dictates.

Large Flat-topped Desk

Components. The desk in Plate 31 is truly an example of "mix and match," since the top is from an altogether different period than the legs. While these legs could probably have been saved for an oak top of similar period, it is unlikely that enough legs could ever be found to match the antique walnut top. It originally had eight legs, all of which had been broken off—some of them completely, others down to splintered stubs.

In fact this top looked so unpromising "before," that it came as a complete surprise, once it was stripped, to see what a lovely piece it must have been. If sometime in the future a set of legs from this particular period can be found, there's always the possibility for a rematch. In the meantime, it's a very attractive desk, with the walnut top and the oak legs finished to blend harmoniously.

The handsome table legs (Plate 13) are those I told you about earlier; they were part of the badly damaged table from a rural Grange hall. While the tabletop was unusable, the ornate legs, after being stripped, were more beautiful than I'd imagined.

Preliminary Steps. Preparatory work on turned oak legs after they're stripped (as well as on a chip-carved center design), can be tedious because it calls for thorough and careful sanding. Since the wood was old and quite dry, a little oil was rubbed into the legs—first a thin coat of natural Danish oil, then a thin coat of a darker, walnut-toned oil until the legs were more nearly the shade of the desk top.

As for the top, I had it commercially stripped because black enamel is particularly hard to remove. Broken parts

Plate 31: Composite desk by the author recycles a walnut top with the oak legs in Plate 13.

of legs remaining on the desk top were sawed off in line with lower edge of the skirting.

The desk top was given a protective coat of satin-finish varnish (no oil). (See below, "Final Finishing.") Touch-ups and color blending were done after the desk was assembled.

Adapting the Legs. One obstacle to overcome in adapting semicircular preassembled legs of this type: they're not *high* enough for desk legs—because originally, as part of a table, they were attached to the glide assembly, a thick laminated wooden block that increased their height by several inches. (Average desk height is from 28½ to 29½ inches.)

The desk top used here combines nicely with these legs for two reasons. First, the preconstructed top with its extra depth gives added height to the legs. And second, the two preassembled leg units placed at an angle, coincide with locations of the desk top's missing legs—except at center front where they're not needed, and on the two back corners. At the back, the leg units curve and bypass both corners. So in order to give the desk a finished, well-balanced look, two 6-inch curtain rod finials—stained to match—are screwed into the back corners from underneath. (Secondhand finials usually have *dowel screws* implanted in them, or you can buy new finials and screws at a hardware store or lumberyard.)

Assembly of Desk. Plate 13 shows how the two sets of legs looked "before" (and upside down) with one wooden brace still attached. On each set of legs, the flat board joining the fancy curved center panel to the two legs was left intact to aid in reconstruction. Edges of each board were smoothed and corners trimmed and rounded so that when placed at an angle they'd fit within the contour of the desk top's underside.

Through holes drilled in these boards, large screws fasten each set of legs to reinforced areas underneath the desk top.

Final Finishing. No oil was used on the top of the desk since it might have further darkened the walnut wood. Instead, four or five coats of low gloss varnish were applied to the top, and fine sandpaper and superfine steel wool used between coats.

On small spots where wood filler was used to patch or fill in, and for lighter areas on the oak legs, additional stain as well as a little burnt umber oil color was rubbed in and allowed to dry thoroughly before adding a coat or two of the satin-finish varnish. (See "Spanish Frame," Chapter 5.)

Plate 32: This rustic kitchen desk by the author was once a built-in set of open shelves salvaged from a remodeling job.

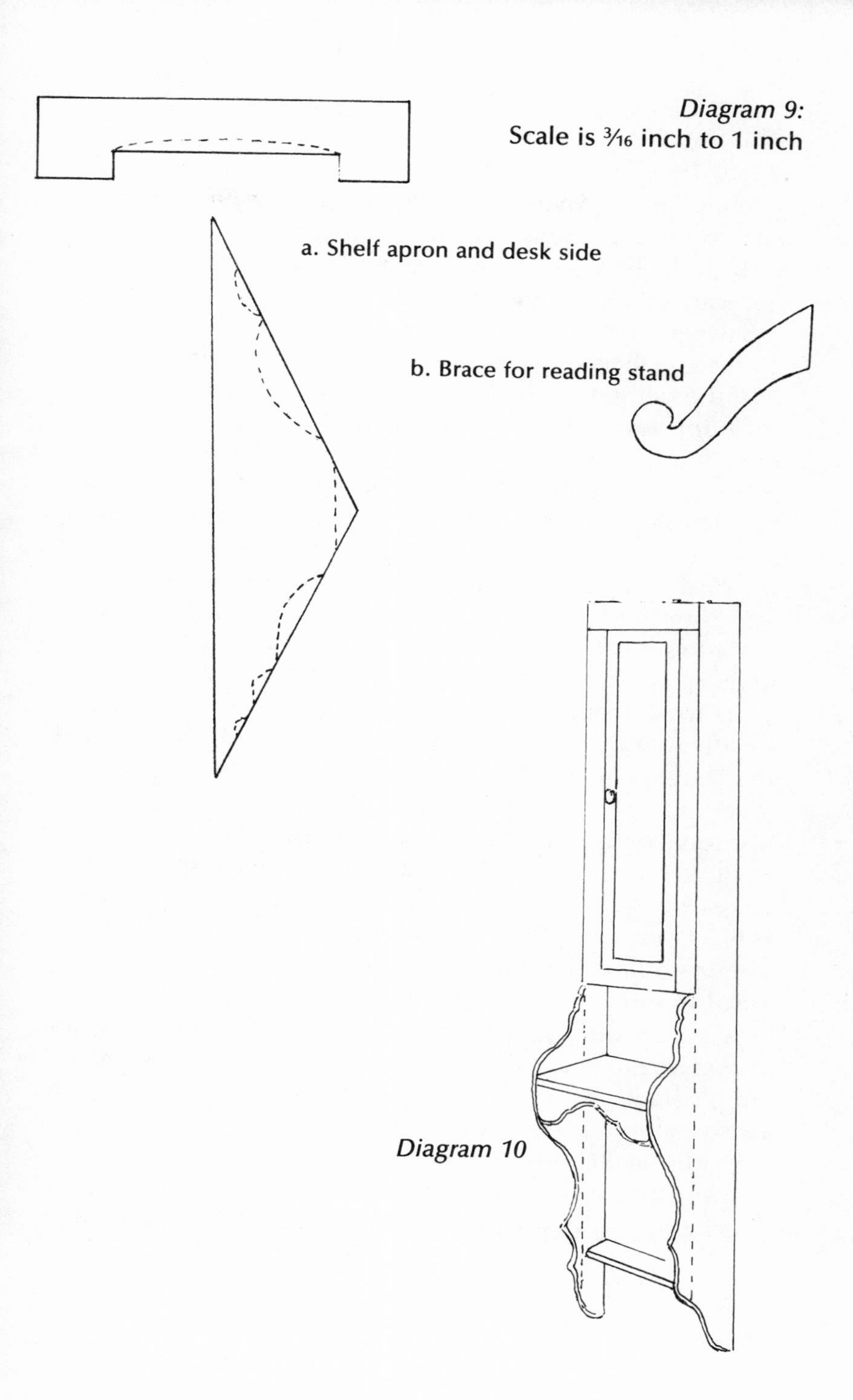
Diagram 9:
Scale is 3⁄16 inch to 1 inch
a. Shelf apron and desk side
b. Brace for reading stand
Diagram 10

Rustic Desk

While it is fun to rebuild with oak or other old hardwood, it is equally rewarding to see what can be done with unlikely pieces made from rough lumber that does not warrant refinishing and must be painted instead.

Salvaged from a remodeling job, a set of 7-foot high by 19-inch wide, open shelves with no backing is transformed into the tall narrow wall desk in Plate 32.

Country primitive in style, the desk is deliberately made to look quaint and hand-built. As a space-saving measure, practical for a kitchen or child's room, the desk is attached to the wall. But it could be converted into a free-standing piece if the bottom edge of the base were extended forward several inches at the front and additional bracing added in the form of wooden blocks along the base.

Writing Shelf Area. Although the finished desk is 6 feet in height, the top cupboard measures only 7½ inches deep from front to back. Therefore, to gain extra depth for the writing shelf, a curved board is glued and doweled to each side board, bringing the shelf depth to 13 inches. (See pattern, Diagrams 9a and 10.) To enlarge pattern, use squared graph paper or paper you've measured and squared yourself. Number both original small squares and larger ones (1, 2, 3, 4, etc.) across the top and down the side. Then reproduce on a larger scale in each of the larger squares the lines that appear in the corresponding small square.)

A cardboard pattern is cut to approximate angle of curves needed for shelf-support area, starting with the simple basic outlines for sidepieces and shelf apron shown by solid lines in Diagram 9a.

Additional curves in the wood are worked out the same as were those for the coatrack in Chapter 2. Angles or notches are cut with a saw, then rounded and shaped using a wood rasp and sandpaper. Since the curves are mostly contained in the added-on pieces, primary shaping is done before these are joined to the shelf and side boards. A final touch-up with wood rasp and sandpaper is done after these boards are glued together. A couple of holes are also drilled in each back edge of the two supplementary boards, and wooden dowels are set into them before joining to the side boards, in which corresponding dowel holes have been drilled. This is not a must, but it does add strength to the desk—particularly since it's in the stress-area of the writing shelf.

Underneath the shelf, a narrow strip of wood is glued and tacked to each long upright board (extending from back of desk and almost to front edge of added-on section) as extra support for the writing shelf. Cut strips a trifle short to allow room for attaching the shelf apron.

Top. The hinged cupboard door is a salvaged frame without glass. It was originally a glassed door used horizontally on the front of an old stacked bookcase. (I found three unmatched ones, minus their glass, at a sale.)

The door is placed on the cupboard so its top rests against *half* of the top shelf's front edge, which serves as a stop for the door when it's closed. The other half of the shelf's edge forms a brace for the cupboard's fancy crown, which is nailed to the shelf and glued to the cupboard as well.

The top of the cuboard is sawed off even with the crown. Subtracting this cutoff portion and the few inches trimmed off in tapering the bottom, the original 7-foot height of the shelves comes down to approximately 6 feet for the completed desk.

Finishing. A gathered curtain is used on the door in place of glass. The desk is finished in yellow and lightly antiqued with umber.

Painted Wall Desk

The wall-hung desk/buffet shown in Plate 12 was an oblong table with two Duncan Phyfe pedestal legs (one broken) when it was acquired.

A narrow decorative backboard was attached along the back edge to make it look more like a desk.

Brackets. The handsome old pair of cast-iron brackets was acquired at a bargain price because a 2-inch tip had been broken off of one of them. The other was cut off to match with a hacksaw, edges of the brackets filed smooth and both of them painted with wrought-iron black (satin black) spray paint. (Black hardware complements the brackets.) Careful measuring is necessary in attaching heavy brackets of this type to a wall—not only to expedite the location of studs (at 16-inch intervals) but to ensure the best possible placement for the desk top.

Selecting Your Material

To further illustrate how versatile are these portions of prebuilt furniture, many of the parts used to construct desks in this chapter are interchangeable with those (in Chapters 10 and 11) that are utilized for cupboards, chests, bookcases and display cabinets. This gives you more options for every piece of material—to test, try, and consider in planning a "mix and match" transformation.

9

The Leftovers

A spraddle-legged table/lamp combination with a 2-foot length of lamp rod protruding from the tabletop was one of the less promising castoffs I've seen. Nevertheless, there are usable building parts even in an unlikely discard such as this. The flat boards that form the table top and the lower shelf, of the same size as the top, are adaptable as backboards for wall pieces or as tops for bookcases and display cabinets.

Surprisingly, the legs also have possibilities; they might prove useful in a project that calls for thick blocks of wood or a sturdy brace.

Unexpected Dividends

These further examples of semimodern uglies frequently found in thrift stores confirm that few things indeed are hopeless.

Bookcase Headboards

A bed headboard with a built-in bookshelf was given a new life as a wall cupboard by salvaging the top portion including the shelf. A paper pattern was cut to facilitate further shaping of the backboard along the bottom edge where it was sawed off. Part of another headboard forms the crown for the cupboard in Plate 33.

Step-Type End Tables

The wooden portion of the bookstand in Plate 34 is constructed from a broken leather-topped end table. For directions, see Chapter 12, under "Book Stand with Metal Legs."

Tabletop Record Players

These make fine sewing boxes (attractive gifts), especially if the case is wood. The record-playing mechanism is removed, holes are filled and the box painted, antiqued and lined with pretty wallpaper or fabric.

Television Cabinets

A common item found in thrift stores today is the discarded television set. Since we're interested not in the TV itself but in the cabinet, the trick lies in finding one with a salvageable cabinet and a TV that is inoperative, or nearly so. Otherwise, the recycling becomes too expensive to be practical.

Contemporary open-front TV sets are apt to be made of synthetic materials. Even so, the prefabricated framework of such a cabinet makes a good start for a cupboard. And you might consider using two similar cabinets, one on top of the other. Directions for reconstructing an older type TV cabinet are included in Chapter 10.

TV Stands

Another product of the television salvage market is the

Plate 33: Tall cupboard recycled by the author from an old TV cabinet, cut in two.

TV stand—not the metal kind (unfortunately, since there are millions of them) but the older ones made of wood. These are usually hardwood, so consider them potential building material even if they're just a set of legs with crosspieces to form a frame.

Side braces are screwed into legs with double-pointed screws. Remove these braces first. The legs are doweled into the front and back braces. Clamp brace in vise and knock apart by rapping inner sides of legs with a hammer.

Granted, you're not likely to turn these castoffs or others like them into heirloom pieces, but they *can*

Plate 34: Book stand by the author combines secondhand table parts with a cast-iron footstool base.

become a source of building material for some attractive and useful furniture.

Note: When buying these and other types of less desirable salvage, don't pay too high a price. And check carefully beforehand to see if the wood is modified, i.e., fiberboard, particle board, chipboard, or plywood with a plastic coating. Finishes are deceptive and can look amazingly like the real thing.

If cupboard doors turn out to be modified wood, they can give you trouble when it comes to drilling holes for screws or attaching hardware, particularly hinges, which may not hold.

Imitation hardwood cupboard doors, however, are sometimes most attractive and can be used as backing for a wall piece or as a decorative facing for a planter. So if you inadvertently buy some, don't throw them away.

Turntable-Type TV Stands

Many of the older TV stands are low wooden tables with a turntable top. These are much too useful the way they are to take them apart for building components. In my basement work area, I use one of these stands as a combination sawhorse and work table. It is low—just the right height on which to lay a board for sawing. Not only that, but the whole tabletop turns around, adjusting to whatever angle is handy, and is unsurpassed as a place to do painting or antiquing, because you can turn your work as necessary without moving out of your tracks.

Veneered Buffet

Dealers may shy away from a piece such as the buffet in Diagram 11a because it won't bring a good price, and it's too large and heavy to handle or display with ease.

Refinishing can also be difficult, if not impossible, because the sides, top and drawer fronts are veneered.

These buffets date back to the thirties and may show a good deal of wear—at least on the top—so they often sell at quite reasonable prices. I bought the one in Diagram 11a for fifteen dollars and have seen them priced lower than that.

Despite the veneer, this is a very solid, serviceable piece of furniture. The drawers glide perfectly, bottoms, sides and back are all solid oak—yet the entire chest is veneered. Oak on top of oak! Imagine! Cabinet construction of the period favored wood grains that were extremely uniform; therefore, hardwood was often overlaid with a fine-grained veneer.

Liabilities

The top of this buffet was deeply stained and a trifle chipped along the back. There were no large damaged areas on the chest itself except for an occasional shabby place where the varnish was worn. There were also no spots where the veneer had peeled, other than a few small chips along the edges; these I carefully sanded.

The wooden drawer pulls—oak with a brass center—could have been quite nice, on something else, but gave this chest a clunky, uninteresting look.

Positive Aspects

In addition to being solidly built, other assets of this particular buffet include a compartmented top drawer 55 inches long, lined with a soft purple fabric—the kind used in silverware chests. The deeper drawers are ideal for storing tablecloths or linens, and the two side cabinets, dishes.

Obviously, the practical features of this storage chest warrant some effort toward renovation. So let's see what

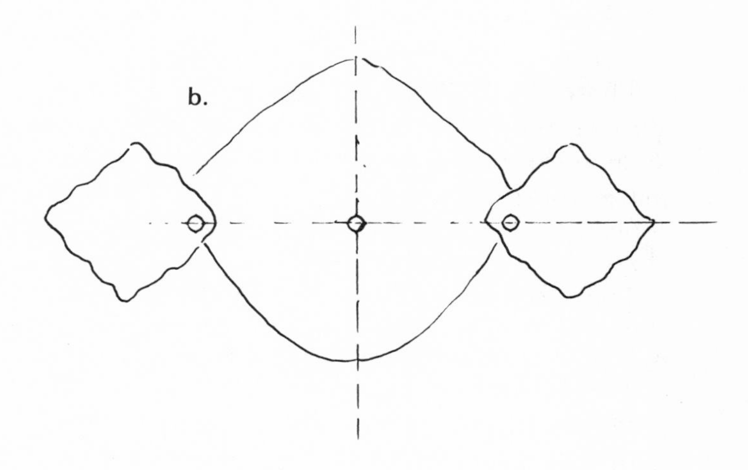

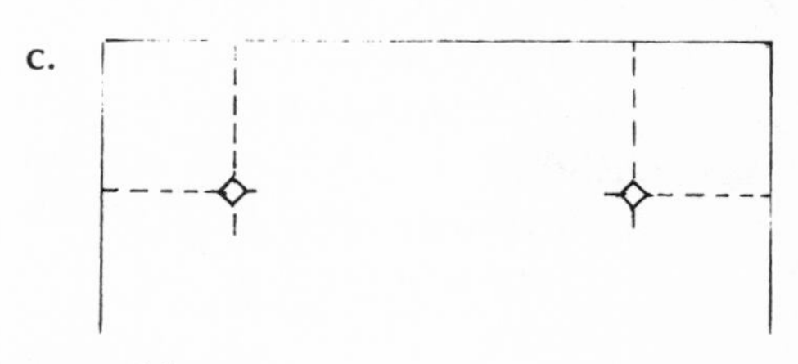

Diagram 11

can be done to minimize its liabilities without a great expenditure of time or money.

To Repair a Damaged Top. If veneer is loose along the edge, reglue and weight down until dry. To repair veneer that has loosened and raised in the center, slit bubbled area with a razor blade, insert glue, press from both sides toward the center slit. Wipe off excess glue and apply pressure over area until glue dries.

You can buy thin sheets of veneer of various kinds of wood from woodworking specialty houses (an item usually included in their catalog merchandise). (See Chapter 3, list of catalogs.)

However, it doesn't always pay to reveneer a chest or table with a ruined top, if the piece of furniture is not all that good to begin with.

Alternative Solutions: the Cover-up. A long frameless mirror, cut to size or slightly smaller, can be used to top a chest of this kind. (This treatment is particularly suited to a dining room buffet.) Or you might use mirrored tiles, preferably not gued to the buffet itself but to a thin sheet of wood edged with molding.

A pretty fabric covered with a cut-to-size piece of heavy glass is another possibility. As a more or less temporary solution, I covered the damaged top of the buffet with an antique tablecloth.

To Renovate Finish on Front and Sides. First of all, try a good washing. Use a damp, not wet, cloth and rub it freely over a bar of mild soap; wash surfaces well, then wipe with a freshly dampened cloth until all traces of soap are removed. When dry, use superfine steel wool wherever the varnish is worn or shabby. Wipe surface with a cloth barely moistened in paint thinner, then apply a light coat of low gloss varnish—over the damaged area only. After

Plate 35: A large, rather old buffet, inexpensively refurbished by the author, utilizes new brass hardware spray-painted black.

this is dry, apply a second coat over the entire drawer front or whatever area you're working on.

Replacing Hardware. The buffet's black hardware (see Plate 35) is a combination of new metal drawer pulls and back plates, or escutcheons—both available at home improvement stores or hardware stores that cater to the do-it-yourselfer—plus a couple of garage sale pieces of ornate pot metal used as back plates on the two doors.

It is extremely difficult to find good-looking black hardware. Since the drawer pulls and the escutcheons were available only in a brass finish, I covered them with a coat of wrought iron black (satin black) spray paint.

The fancy back plates (escutcheons) conceal existing holes in the buffet where knobs were originally attached. Each new drawer handle is placed slightly below the back plate, but with its ends just touching it, so that when the hardware is assembled, handle and back plate appear to be all in one piece. To attach handles:

1. Make a pattern, or template, out of lightweight cardboard such as a file card. Trace around escutcheon and handle (drawer pull) ends, but not the handle itself, and mark mounting holes—so your pattern will look something like Diagram 11b.
2. Fasten escutcheons temporarily in place on the drawer front with metal screws (provided in package for this purpose) through center hole in plate, and existing hole in drawer where the knob was attached.
3. Place handle in proper position touching plate, mark location of ends of handle on drawer. Measure down from top and over from side of drawer front as in Diagram 11c, to determine approximate location of center point of each handle. (This can be adjusted slightly—one way or the other—when handles are attached, to ensure that handles and plates are touching.)
4. Fold handle pattern with ends together, mark center

of pattern. Match center of pattern to each center-point mark on drawer front and mark locations for holes.

5. Drill holes in drawer front for attaching handles. (Start each hole with a nail.)

6. Attach handles from inside drawer front with metal screws provided in package.

Escutcheons. The escutcheons are added last. Each of these decorative metal plates has a tiny projecting prong underneath on one side to keep it from turning around—since escutcheons are fastened with only one screw at the center.

1. To cope with this projection, lay the escutcheon in place on the drawer front and rap with a hammer to mark location of prong on drawer. Then pound in the point of a nail—twisting it back and forth and around—to enlarge the hole enough so that the prong can be recessed.

2. Fasten escutcheon in place on drawer using provided threaded metal screw and nut. Spray a little black paint into a jar lid, and use a tiny brush to paint screw heads black. Touch up any installation mars or scratches on hardware. Finally, for added durability, cover all hardware with a light coat of satin-finish varnish.

Somebody's Mistakes

Chests with Sawed-Off Legs

While junking I run across a great many chests and tables with sawed-off legs—some of them lovely old pieces except for that one overwhelming flaw. An idea for renovating these ruined chests came to me while stripping an old oak desk which was built solid down to the floor: why not conceal the legs behind a board—build skirting to enclose them so that the new bottom of the chest is flush with the floor like the desk?

Diagram 2 shows a chest with cutoff legs as it looked

Plate 36: Chest with sawed-off legs, remodeled and refinished. Shown "before" in Diagram 2.

"before," and illustrates the reconstruction used to alter its appearance. The finished piece is shown in Plate 36.(The drawer pulls are new reproductions, attached from inside the drawers.)

In the course of pondering what I could use that would serve as skirting to enclose the stubby legs, I remembered saving portions of two old tables with ruined tops, and these yielded three hardwood boards of adequate size and thickness.

To Enclose Legs. Leave the sawed-off legs exactly as they are; they can serve as braces for the skirting.

1. Two side boards are measured and cut to the exact depth of the chest from front to back. These overlap the bottom board on the chest and extend downward to the floor to enclose the legs. (If legs are extremely short, allow board to project beyond them.)
2. A line is marked on the underside of the skirting, and, if chest is paneled as this one was, the skirting board is notched out (with a chisel and an X-acto knife) along this line to accommodate high- and low-relief areas of chest's bottom board.
3. Holes for screws are drilled and counterbored at points marked in Diagram 2.
4. After side skirting is attached, the front skirting is measured and cut to the width of the chest, plus thickness of the skirting on both sides.
5. The front skirting is drilled and counterbored for screws, and attached.
6. Wooden hole plugs are glued over all screw heads.

A Table with Ruined Top and Legs

A sorry result of careless remodeling is the topless oak table with sawed-off legs shown in Plate 14. When bought at a garage sale it had a nailed-on plywood top, covered with linoleum. Plate 37 shows this table recycled. For more about this piece, see Chapter 11.

Disassembling Old Furniture

Table

Do you recall, in Chapter 3, the battered old table whose oak legs were salvaged and used to build the desk in Plate 31?

While disassembling this table, I learned how solidly furniture was put together in that bygone era when things

Plate 37: Base section for the two-part bookcase (Plate 40) uses the table shown in Plate 14 turned upside down.

were built to last. In addition to the table's being made of solid oak, its assembly employed a great many screws and bolts, hardwood braces and corner blocks.

The table was taken apart by first removing all visible screws, then knocking out glued and/or nailed blocks with a hammer.

To remove a nail that won't budge—in old hardwood they can be exasperatingly difficult—clamp the *nail* in a vise, then pry it out by manipulating the board.

When a nail breaks off in the wood without enough left exposed to grip for pulling, use a nail set to sink it below the surface, and putty over the top with a wood filler.

If rusty bolts and screws prove resistant when taking apart old furniture, spray rusted parts with WD-40, then wait a bit before trying to remove them. Conversely, for *tightening* a screw in hard or old wood, grease the screw first with petroleum jelly.

Sewing Machine Cabinet

The cabinet in Plate 24 was fairly easy to take apart because the glue had deteriorated to a point where even the center panels in the sides and in the back of the cabinet were loosened. These panels needed realigning and regluing before the sides could be made over into something else. (See directions for regluing, Chapter 7, under "Oak Wall Planter.")

Chairs (Seats, Backs, Legs)

Last spring I visited a friend who lives on a farm in Indiana. She gave me a pretty cupboard crown which I carried wrapped in paper on the plane back to Oregon.

The rest of my Indiana treasures consisted of unrelated parts and pieces of broken chairs retrieved from the uppermost corner of the barn loft. These I packed in a box and brought home along with my suitcase in the baggage compartment of the plane.

In the process of disassembling these chair sections, I found they were put together with dowels and lots of screws (sometimes extra ones had been added to reinforce broken joints). Occasionally, where a screw was rusted or impossible to remove, I sawed it through with a hacksaw. I also salvaged parts of rungs, spindles and legs since they too were oak.

Parts and Pieces. Besides utilizing such parts for repairing old chairs, there are other possibilities. Plain chair back spindles are used to reconstruct missing parts in oak

Plate 38: Chair-back reading stand designed by the author.

furniture and as oak dowels for rebuilding. Fancy turned spindles are recycled as ornamentation.

The wall piece described in Chapter 6 (Plate 21) utilizes an old desk chair seat which is grooved on the top surface for caning and put together with the front section doweled into side pieces. Most dining chairs are constructed in exactly the same way. The preassembled front portions of the seats are adaptable as shelves.

In Plate 38 is a fancy chair back converted into a reading stand.

A plain chair back can be transformed into a doll bed headboard and the chair legs used as part of the framework construction.

Turned posts ornamenting the wall piece in Plate 5 are leftover legs from a broken chair.

Odds and Ends of Salvage

Brackets. In addition to salvaging small, ready-made wooden brackets similar to those in Diagram 6, all sorts of things can be used to *create* brackets and shelf supports.

For instance, one way to recycle a table pedestal with one leg missing is illustrated in Diagram 8b. The two legs remaining on the pedestal can be made to yield three pairs of small brackets simply by using a square to mark the legs as shown in the diagram (for three right-angled cuts) and saving the brackets apart.

Note: To Saw Thick Boards or Blocks of Hardwood. Carving boards, table and sofa legs, heavy decorative wood, etc.—boards that are solid hardwood make for slow cutting. A power saw would of course simplify the operation. Since I don't have one, I use a good sharp handsaw.

When sawing through any board that is unusually thick or very hard wood, don't try to saw the full distance at one time. Leave the board clamped in the vise and alternate the exertion of sawing with small easy jobs such as gluing.

Do take pains to plainly mark the board (using pencil and a straightedge) so you can see the line as you saw. This will minimize the necessity to even the edge with a wood rasp and sandpaper after it is cut.

Incidentally, a surgical face mask isn't a bad idea if you're doing a lot of sawing in an enclosed area. (Baby departments carry inexpensive, disposable ones.) Also, a tank-type vacuum cleaner is virtually indispensable for keeping your work area free of sawdust and sanding residue.

Wooden Gingerbread. To salvage brittle ornamental wood, and oak gingerbread that is still attached to parts of old furniture, strip off varnish or paint with stripper or TSP (see Chapter 13). Remove bits of trim while still wet by inserting a thin knife behind them and prying gently, easing them up a little at a time. Remove tiny nails or brads with pliers. Wash glue off the back of trim (under the faucet with a brush). Then dry the decorative bits of wood carefully between two pieces of cloth or of a blotter, with weight on top to prevent warping (or lightly clamp in vise between two flat pieces of wood).

You can cut apart or reshape these small bits of carved wood to suit yourself—to make them fit a certain area, or to produce a matched pair for ornamental purposes, or for assembling a group of them to form a larger piece of decorative trim.

Use an X-acto knife with blades suited to the size and shape of the wood. Glue back any small chips that break off. Work carefully, and sand each step of the way.

Preassembled Boards. Occasionally, you'll find an old beveled board that appears unusually thick. It may be *two* boards with rounded edges—a thin board superimposed on a thicker one, with the underneath board a bit larger to give the effect of a bevel.

The top board may be nailed and glued, but often the glue is so old it has let go, or at least it may let go when the piece is stripped.

Note: Conversely, this is also a good way to achieve the beveled look. With a wood rasp, simply round the edges of two boards, one slightly larger than the other, but both of the same shape. Then glue and nail them together for a beveled effect.

The Leftovers

Whether you're pondering the potential in old boards, prefabricated furniture parts, bits of beautiful wood, or unlikely leftovers, start by asking yourself these questions: Is this worth restoring or only good for salvage? How can I get maximum effect with minimum effort and expense?

10

Shortcuts to Restyling Chests and Cupboards

Now let's recycle on a larger scale. Instead of working with odds and ends and parts, we'll go a step further in the use of prefabricated material and put together complete units of ready-built furniture to form a single large piece.

The bottom of the charming composite shown in Plate 2 was once a mahogany-stained thrift store chest. It was adapted as a base and combined with a garage sale cupboard. Both pieces were semi-old and had broken panels in the doors and missing hardware.

As you can see, the now elegant finished cupboard gives no hint of having been two unrelated pieces of secondhand furniture.

Paint is part of the transformation. (See Chapter 13.) But happily the woman who assembled this cupboard (see Chapter 1) also combined furniture of unusually compatible design—straight lines and panel construction of the upper cupboard complement similar features on the chest. And the addition of matched brass (reproduction) hardware further unifies the design.

Add or Subtract. The same mix-and-match principle applies here as it did for desks in Chapter 8—desk tops, legs and dividers could be interchanged—except that now larger units of furniture are interchanged. The fun in this kind of reconstruction lies in discovering pieces that coordinate well, and in trying to visualize how a composite piece will look after it has some ornamentation added (or removed) and it is painted, stripped, oiled or refinished.

Size is irrelevant so long as pieces of similar scale are used together. You can think big—even a large old buffet could be adapted in this fashion and transformed into an oversized hutch, if you happened onto a top cupboard or open shelves of similar wide proportions. This in fact would be an excellent solution for a piece with damaged veneer since the surface could be filled or patched, then painted.

Also, if you're looking for more shelf, cupboard and drawer space, one way to get additional storage in a limited area is to fit an occasional *tall* chest or cupboard into your decorating scheme.

At the end of this chapter you will find instructions for transforming an old TV cabinet into a tall cupboard as illustrated in Plate 33.

Here the advantage of recycling for additional height is apparent. Not only do you conserve floor space—and give your decor a lift—thanks to your handsome chest/cupboard creation, you'll find you have room for all those little extras.

The following lists of potential bases, legs and tops offer suggestions for other salvage to transform.

Chest/Cupboard Components

Here are just a few of the items that are adaptable for this purpose:

Prefabricated Bases

Low two-drawer chest
Cabinet with shelves (low or table height)
Buffet
Dresser-height chest with three or more drawers
Oblong tables (with or without sawed-off legs, see Plate 14)
Cabinets from old or antique furniture

You can utilize legs or a supplementary prefabricated base on which to set any of the pieces above for extra height, or to raise it off the floor. Consider the following:

Supplementary Legs and Bases

A thick hardwood frame
Low ready-made furniture base
Leftover legs from tables, sofas, footstools, bookcases and so on.
Skirting (built down flush to the floor to form a base. Consider damaged tabletops as possible material, or wooden bed parts—headboards, footboards or side rails.)

Cupboard Tops

Open shelves
Cupboards with various types of doors
Shelf/drawer combinations

Of course all of these can be dressed up or stripped down to produce an infinite variety of designs.

Cupboards, Renovated and Restyled

Shelves. To install shelves in an open cupboard frame—if original shelves are unsalvageable or missing altogether—lay cupboard on its side. Measure and mark a line for each shelf on both of the cupboard's inner sides.

Measure and cut shelves the correct width to fit inside cupboard.

Cut ¾-inch molding (for shelf supports) to slightly *less* than the depth of the cupboard. Glue, and tack molding with small brads to cupboard sides, checking with one of the shelf boards as you go along to be sure both supports are at the same height so shelf will be level. Lay shelves on installed molding strips.

In some cases, *covered* shelves may be the answer. If you have a hardwood cupboard that does not have shelves, and you lack the material to make them, here is a camouflage ploy that will solve the problem while you're waiting to find the right kind of shelf boards.

Cut shelves from ½-inch plywood. Then cover them with oilcloth, fabric or wallpaper—oilcloth works well for hang-down scallops since it has stiffness and body and is less apt to curl or appear limp.

In searching out material, don't pass up old cupboards that appear hopeless. The refinished one shown in Plate 39 was one of the worst looking I've ever seen. It had coats and coats of chipped paint, alternating with four or five layers of glued-on wallpaper, oilcloth—even Christmas wrapping paper. In addition, the cupboard was constructed from very rough lumber, and the two doors' missing panels had been replaced with cardboard.

After the various coatings were stripped away, the backing nailed down and wooden panels added, the cupboard was given an aged-pine finish designed to minimize the effects of wear and neglect. It now functions again in its original capacity as a top for a "kitchen queen."

Chests, Restyled or Refurbished

A word of caution: in the beginning, it's better not to

Plate 39: A battered old cupboard top is shown restored with (Puritan) pine finish. Pattern on glass (set into cupboard doors) was sandblasted. Restoration done by Eric Mahata, proprietor of The Big Dipper—a stripping service in Sellwood, Oregon.

Plate 40: Large armoire-type bookcase by the author has ornate added trim. The bookcase, in two parts, is set on a separate base (Plate 37). Accessories by Ethel Rohrer and Nancy Egge.

attempt building in whole sets of drawers. Prefabricated or not, this demands patience and a certain amount of skill. At first, enlist the aid of a carpenter. Or wait till you've taken apart some furniture and observed the different types of drawer glides, how they're constructed and the way they work—then you'll be ready to try it on your own.

Let's take the reconstructed chest with sawed-off legs that was described in Chapter 9 (Plate 36), and picture it restyled with the addition of carved wooden (reproduction) drawer pulls and, on the drawer fronts, some narrow molding finished in the same dark tone as the pulls.

If you were to substitute a chest of this type for the upside-down-table base in Plate 40, then add doors to its top cupboard, restyling could be carried a step further, resulting in a piece reminiscent of an old wardrobe or armoire.

In keeping with the chest's wooden pulls and trim, dark-toned knobs and molding might also be used on the cupboard doors.

To Cut Molding. You can use either a metal miter box or a simple wooden one (available at variety and hardware stores) to cut the molding at a 45-degree angle. In some areas there are do-it-yourself picture framing shops; they have an excellent selection of moldings for sale. The metal corner braces used in these shops are an inexpensive hardware item and an invaluable aid for assembling angled corners.

If you yourself put together a frame, or watch someone else do one, the whole mitering process will be easily understood.

Wood or Metal Trim and Hardware

The selection of hardware plays an important part in any restyling project. And part of the fun is discovering odd bits of wood or metal that you can adapt for this purpose.

Keep an eye out for large embossed pieces of ornamental brass—or jewelry—that would combine well with chunks of decorative wood or metal; anything that might serve as drawer pulls, handles, trim or back plates.

Old Brass. To refurbish old or very tarnished hardware, polish high spots in the design with a scouring pad or superfine steel wool. Leave the deeper indentations dark and unpolished for depth and contrast. Finally, touch up the high spots with a soft cloth and a cream type polish. (I like the kind that comes in a tube. Try the sporting goods department; fishermen use this type of polish for brass spinners.)

Remember, there's a marvelous array of reproduction hardware available too, and some of it is solid brass.

How to Age New Brass. Suppose you buy some lovely copies of old brass drawer pulls, yet they appear garish and raw—not truly antique. You can age shiny new drawer pulls, escutcheons, coat hooks, and make them look like antique ones.

As a rule, reproductions of old brass hardware are not lacquered, so you won't need to strip them first. (Should it prove necessary to remove lacquer, strip with TSP or sal soda, see Chapter 13.)

There are kits available for darkening brass (see catalog list in Chapter 3), or buy a few ounces of *liver of sulfur* (in dry lump form) at a pharmacy. Dissolve it in a small amount of water, using enough liver of sulfur to produce a fairly strong solution that is greenish in color. Store in a tightly covered container, as the mixture has an unpleasant sulfurous odor. Use a small inexpensive child's paint brush to paint solution on the brass, going over grooved or indented areas in the design several times. (For some reason, this works better than soaking the brass in a solution.)

Allow hardware to dry, and repeat process if more oxidation is required. Rinse under faucet, and dry.

Unless you put a coat of lacquer on brass, it continues to oxidize until it eventually needs polishing again. Personally, I like it that way, but you may prefer to lacquer yours, because in time the brass develops deeper spots of oxidation that could require professional buffing.

To Lacquer Brass. Clear nail polish works fine for very small pieces of brass; larger ones look better covered with metal lacquer. This goes a long way, so buy a small can. Avoid spray lacquer.

Be sure the brass pieces are thoroughly dry; set them in a warm place, as on an oven door with heat turned low. Lacquer goes on better if applied when metal is warm.

Use a small brush with light-colored bristles, and flow lacquer on *quickly* and *evenly*. Watch for runs, but avoid rebrushing if possible as this kind of lacquer dries almost instantly. Set brass on oven door to dry or in a warm dust-free place. In some cases, even *brass* hardware looks richer with a dark finish. For instance, the door hardware that was on the TV cabinet mentioned earlier is used in its original oxidized state to set off the Swedish blue of the reconstructed tall cupboard in Plate 33.

Tall Cupboard (from an Old TV Cabinet)

In the not-so-far-off future when television sets are built into the walls, TV cabinets may become a thing of the past. They are now fairly plentiful at thrift stores and garage sales, and these cabinets—particularly the older models—although seldom made from high-quality material, can be turned into useful, attractive furniture with good storage potential. The biggest drawback in utilizing a vintage cabinet is that it's often too deep for an average-sized cupboard.

If you've saved one of those too-good-to-throw-away cabinets, recycling it can be a rewarding project. On the other hand, if you're buying the outside shell of a TV expressly to rebuild, don't pay too high a price for it even if it's old—there are other things you can use to build a combination cupboard of comparable size. Alternative materials might include secondhand cupboards, cabinets or shelves with similar cut-down possibilities, or plainly styled unfinished furniture that you can mix and match or upgrade with new or used doors, feet, hardware or trim.

Reconstruction will vary according to the type of cabinet, but we'll cover the basic steps needed for rebuilding an older style cabinet into a tall cupboard similar to the one shown in Plate 33.

Preparation of Cabinet. Eliminate all TV and electrical components *(avoid breaking the picture tube; it contains a gas).* Remove any panels or speakers that can be unscrewed or lifted out.

Remove casters or glides from back half of cabinet and reposition them on back edge of front half (which will become the base of your cupboard). If necessary, glue on a wood block to support a caster centered at the back.

Some cabinets have cross-braces (to support the picture tube); the one used here had a plywood shelf with irregular cutout areas which I left in place, since it was impossible to remove without disassembling the cabinet, and later covered with another shelf board.

Braces (if needed). Before you start sawing, check to see that the back half of the cabinet is adequately supported inside to prevent it falling apart. Add more bracing if necessary—it need be nothing more than a couple of 1-inch by 2-inch strips glued to the cabinet's inner walls. Cut two pieces of scrap lumber to fit inside the cabinet from back to front. Sand them, then glue and clamp one to each cabinet side (where they can also serve later on as shelf supports). You'll saw through these braces when cutting the cabinet in two; therefore, after the glue has dried, drill holes and fasten these wooden strips with two screws, midway, but avoiding your saw line. (Leave ends free of screws for installing cupboard facing and backing.) Drill into these strips from the outside of the cabinet, enlarging the holes enough to countersink heads of screws so you can putty over them before painting.

Next, cut a crosspiece that will fit the width of the cabinet between its sides. Cut it a bit long, using your wood rasp and sandpaper to achieve a good close fit. Place ends of this crosspiece directly above or below the glued-on side braces—butting them firmly into side braces—and glue. Allow glue to dry, then drill into ends of crosspiece from outside of cabinet and fasten each end in place with a screw.

To Cut Cabinet in Half. Lay cabinet on its side and measure carefully—from the back, since that edge has no projections or trim. At half the cabinet's depth (see *Note),* mark every few inches along one entire side. Turn the cabinet over and do the same along the opposite side, then the top. (The three series of marks should join perfectly into a continuous line around top and sides.)

Note: The cabinet need not be cut exactly in half, so long as what will be the lower cupboard has more depth to it than what will be the top one. A slight setback of the upper cupboard will not detract from the design, and it may be necessary to measure this way in order to avoid sawing *lengthwise* through an inside brace or crosspiece. (Although a brace may run parallel to your saw line and even serve as a guide, it should not be so close that you'll saw into it.)

Now, using a steel rule (or a board) for a straightedge, line it up along your marks. This is where you will saw the cabinet in half, so instead of marking it with a pencil, scratch a visible line in the varnish with a knife or screwdriver—one that will be easy to follow. Mark a line down both sides and across the top of the cabinet, making sure the lines meet at the corners.

Lay cabinet on one side. Using a good sharp saw, start your cut at the bottom edge of the opposite side—which has been placed in position for sawing—and continue to the top. Take care to stay on the line by exerting pressure on the saw in one direction or the other. Divide sawing procedure into several easy stages—leave saw in place and rest as necessary.

If cabinet has a center shelf, saw straight through it as you go, but only enough to clear your way; leave sawing of the rest of shelf to do later. Turn the cabinet over and repeat the process on the other side. Then do the top. Finish sawing through the center shelf last.

A Single Cabinet Has Now Become Two. At this point, your cabinet—two separate parts without backs—will not appear promising, particularly the back half. But look at it this way; each piece (the back as well as the front) is a reinforced, prebuilt outer shell for a cupboard. Think how much framing work these prefabricated parts can save. All you need do to finish them is glue in wooden strips for shelf supports, and face the front of the upper cupboard, or back half, with strips of wood, and add some kind of trim at the top, such as the arched crown (from the center section of a garage sale bed headboard).

Note: Obviously, the upper cupboard—back portion of the cabinet—does require more rebuilding than the lower. So if you decide to utilize only the front part—perhaps using it in a hallway as a space-saving credenza with a mirror above—it's a simple matter to add shelves and backing to the front half only.

To Measure and Cut Shelves. If you haven't any boards on hand, ⅜-inch plywood with wooden strips or molding glued along the front edge will do nicely. Notch out for projections inside cupboards (make paper pattern first).

Backing for Cupboards. To back the two cupboards, I used thin paneling (new), but turned it so the back of the paneling showed inside the cupboards, thus eliminating the need to center its randomly spaced grooved lines. *Do not nail backing in place until both cupboards are completed, to allow access for construction of the shelves and facing.*

To Face Front of Cupboard. Set your cupboard on a low table or somewhere at eye level so you can sit down while you work. I used two ½-inch by 1½-inch strips of new wood to frame the sides, but measure and cut any boards that will fit your particular cabinet (preferably not good hardwood, however, for a cupboard that will be painted). See below, under *Crown,* before measuring.

Tack the strips lightly to the face of the cupboard while you drill holes for screws. Since the walls of the cabinet are thin, drill through the facing strips and into the end of each shelf support. Countersink screws just enough so you can putty over them. At this point, I also glued an extra block of wood in the middle on each side at the top, as backing for the crown.

Make a paper pattern to measure, then cut bottom board to fit exactly between the side facings. Like the crown, this board is attached with screws (from inside) to wooden blocks glued onto the framework.

Crown. If you're going to add a crown of some sort the wooden strips facing each side of the cupboard should end about 3 inches from the top. Since the curved top was oddly shaped on this particular cupboard, I fastened a plain thin board behind the crown first—to add support—and attached this to the wooden blocks with glue and screws.

To Join Cupboards. The two sections, upper and lower, are bolted together. Holes for ¼-inch bolts are drilled in the two bottom front corners and center back of the top section, and corresponding holes in the top of the base cabinet. Bolts are secured with hexagon nuts, which can be unscrewed so the two cabinet sections can be taken apart for moving.

Note: Also, if at any time you decide to create two separate pieces of furniture from the single cupboard, you'll have a bottom section which might be used in an entrance hall with a mirror above, while the upper portion, with feet added, becomes a free-standing bookcase—either with or without the addition of doors. Feet for the bookcase are first attached to a piece of plywood cut to fit its bottom, so that the screws can be removed and the feet taken off for later recombination of the bookcase into other furniture arrangements.

Nailing Shelves and Backing. All shelves are nailed into place with small finishing nails, except for the bottom one in the top cupboard. This is left loose so it can be lifted to attach or remove the bolts that join the two cupboards.

Sand the backing before it is nailed in place since the rougher side will be exposed inside the cupboard.

Trim and Finishing. The TV control panel was removed by making a saw cut down each side, then using a chisel and hammer across the bottom to split it with the grain of the wood. Cut edges are concealed behind a scrolled trim (part of a knickknack shelf) installed over the area where the panel had been.

Note: If knobs and control buttons are removed, the panel can be left in place and covered with decorative wood.

In the upper cupboard, the shelf that was laid over the TV support shelf is similarly treated—not only as a cover-up, but to help unify the design of the piece by more or less repeating the lower shelf trim.

Decorative molding is used around the lower edge of the upper cupboard to fill excess space and create a smoother joining between upper and lower cabinets.

Nails are countersunk and all holes and cracks are filled with putty (add trim to conceal larger ones if necessary). Following the grain of the wood, varnished areas are sanded just enough to reduce gloss before adding a base coat of paint.

The entire cupboard is finished, inside and out, in Swedish blue (use a bright Dutch blue, antiqued with Payne's grey. Also, see Chapter 13, under "Antiquing in Stages"). For a different effect, you might try wallpapering the interior of the cupboard.

As you work along you'll think of new ways to finish or trim your creations, and develop better ways of assembling your projects as well—so experiment, to discover new systems that work best for you.

11

Bookcases and Display Cabinets

Have you a weakness for books? Do you collect coins or figurines? Colored glass? Part of the joy of collecting is sharing that interest with others. And what better showcase to house your special things than one you've designed and built to please yourself.

Large Composite Bookcase (in Two Parts)

Top. When it was bought in a thrift store, the top portion of the bookcase shown in Plate 40 was a battered old cupboard with peeling varnish and ¾-inch plywood slats roughly nailed to its oak sides.

The plywood—evidently added to support shelves that were long gone—was removed and the cupboard stripped. The boards that backed the cupboard, thin and brittle with age, showed large cracks and were badly warped. These were carefully nailed down and narrow slats tacked over the cracks.

Base. The table with sawed-off legs in Plate 14 is used upside down as a base (Plate 37). Salvaged wooden feet, possibly from an old sofa, are glued and doweled into the upside-down tabletop's four corners, emphasizing that it is indeed a base, and raising it 4 inches off the floor to add balance to the design.

To close in the sides, a cardboard pattern is made first, then a ⅝-inch oak board (from a table leaf) is cut, following the pattern, to fit exactly between the front and back legs on either side. These boards are glued into place, and wooden crosspieces attached inside the unit for reinforcement.

Note: If power tools are available, grooves can be cut on the inside of the legs with a router to accommodate thinner, cutdown extensions on the side boards, thus forming mortise and tenon joints.

A prejoined board salvaged from a secondhand pine cabinet tops the base section. Alternative material might include usable portions of a tabletop or oak table leaf, cut to the proper length, doweled and glued together and the edges rounded with a wood rasp. Or, if oak is not available, some other kind of wood might be used.

Since my building material did not yield a wide oak board that was long enough to top the base, I made do with the prefabricated pine board, cut to fit and edged with salvaged oak molding. The top is fastened to the four upside-down table legs with long screws. And once the cupboard is placed atop this preassembled base it leaves only a narrow offset of pine showing—this is stained to match the oak.

The base is backed and floored (at point where legs intersect edge of table apron), using oak paneling from a bed headboard.

Placement of Bookcase and Trim. The two beautiful sections of carved wood framing the upper part of the bookcase are old mirror supports. These had been stored beneath a porch and, though badly weathered, the wood had been protected by several coats of varnish and was still in usable condition once the pieces were stripped. Each is attached with glue and five wooden dowels; (3/8-inch holes are drilled in side and top edges of the heavy ornate wood and corresponding ones in the bookcase.)

The cupboard is placed on top of the base, an equal distance from either side and lined up even with the back. Molding is cut to fit around the bottom of the cupboard, minimizing the 3-inch offset of the base. In order to facilitate moving and combination (interchanging with other tops and bases), these two large units are not fastened together permanently.

Shelves. It is not easy to find oak shelves for a bookcase of this depth. (Table leaves are too narrow unless joinings are made to add more width.) To solve the problem in this particular case, shelves cut from other kinds of wood are stained to match, and each shelf is faced with a strip of salvaged oak molding to achieve a uniform effect.

Tiny metal shelf supports—often used in old bookcases and still available in hardware stores—are inserted into holes in side walls of the cupboard, eliminating the need for wooden shelf supports.

Finishing. After a thorough sanding the completed bookcase was oiled, wiped off, allowed to dry and the entire bookcase then given a thin coat of varnish. Since most of the components are oak—fairly light and uniform in tone—*natural* Danish oil was used.

Display Cabinet/Drawer Combination

For dramatic impact try teaming up the unexpected. In Plate 10, the base with Queen Anne legs—an old phono-

Diagram 12

graph cabinet minus its top and doors (see Diagram 12)—is combined with part of a sewing cabinet, and a turn-of-the-century mirror frame.

Base. A salvaged desk top is cut to size to fit top of phonograph cabinet but not attached permanently until reconstruction of the open-fronted cabinet is completed (to allow access for rebuilding inside the cabinet). For final installation of the top, drill holes through it in each corner, countersink screw, and cover heads with putty.

All four legs are sawed off the small sewing cabinet shown "before" in Plate 9 and described in Chapter 2. Also, its top is pried off and replaced in line with the drawer fronts (or you could simply saw off the overhang). The drawers have been slid out of the frame, or carcase, of the cabinet and set aside while the carcase is being installed in the opening in the phonograph cabinet.

To install drawers or doors in an opening is a step-at-a-time process. It involves measuring to see what will fill the space, then trying a variety of boards and prefabricated parts to judge their effect and finally fitting them into place like pieces of a jigsaw puzzle.

Note: This might be a good place to mention that wooden shingles, or shakes, are ideal for *shimming*. (According to the dictionary: shim *n:* a thin wedge of metal, wood, etc., for driving into crevices; shim *vt*: to fill out or bring to a level by inserting a shim or shims.)

Since no two openings are exactly the same, it's a matter of finding the best possible combination to suit your particular project. You can of course reduce the size of an open space by framing it in to fit prefabricated drawers or doors.

On the phonograph cabinet shown here, this was done by installing across the bottom of the opening a 3-inch-high decorative board (shaped like a piece of wide ornamental trim), then devising a raised platform on which to set the legless sewing cabinet. To do this, cut a board the same size as the sewing cabinet's bottom and raise it approximately 2 inches by gluing wooden blocks underneath the board to create a false floor—one that is almost level with the *top* of the framing board.

Note: In rebuilding old furniture or parts, try to use wherever possible any structural details that remain intact. For example, existing screw holes. Or dowels that are firmly implanted—before you saw these off, consider whether or not they can be utilized for reconstruction. A stout wooden dowel at center front in the framework of the phonograph cabinet (Diagram 12) was exactly right for securing the 3-inch framing board.

The sewing cabinet is recessed slightly, framed in with the 3-inch board at the bottom and narrow molding on the sides and fastened to both the raised platform and, from the outside, to the phonograph cabinet (with long screws).

Remember, when you're going to paint a project, holes for screws can be drilled *anywhere,* then concealed with putty.

A door salvaged from a radio/record cabinet is cut to fit snugly in the opening to the right of the drawers. After marking for placement of hinges on the door's right-hand edge and on the cabinet, chisel out shallow areas on both so hinge flaps may be recessed level with the surface of the wood. Attach hinges with small brass screws. (Start holes for screws with a finishing nail or with a very small drill bit.)

Upper Frame and Shelf. Back corners of the phonograph cabinet's top are cut out slightly to recess lower sidepieces of the frame—these frame extensions are joined to the cabinet back with four large screws, two on each side.

A high shelf topped with curtain rod finials and curved to repeat similar lines on the front of the cabinet is notched out on either side to fit within the open frame and is further supported on each side by a bracket attached to the frame.

Open space inside the empty frame provides a background for a variety of decorating possibilities—family photographs, a colorful painting, perhaps a mirror balanced by a pair of candlesticks or some small hanging shelves with plants on them.

Plate 41: Two-part display cabinet by the author is constructed from table legs and pigeonholed desk divider (Plate 42). Cabinet can be disassembled (the molding-trimmed top lifts off, the pigeonholed cabinet and base are not permanently joined) for greater flexibility in recombination of components. Accessories by Lois and Joe Hart, Milwaukie, Oregon.

The curved wooden crown that tops the frame is the front section of an old desk-chair seat. It is attached to the shelf with a wooden dowel at each end. Finials are fastened to the posts with dowel screws.

Hardware and Paint. Before attaching hardware, the finished piece was painted with satin black spray paint. (For more on this see Chapter 14, under "Refurbish or Rebuild?") A small wooden plaque glued to the door echos existing trim at the top of the frame. Two brass lids with holes drilled in them, similar in design but not a matched pair, are used as trim—one, as decoration on the frame, the other superimposed on the wooden plaque on

Plate 42: Components for display cabinet in Plate 41.

the door to serve as a back plate for the brass knob. Knobs used for drawer (and door) pulls are brass feet from an old lamp base and are attached with round head screws.

Display Cabinet

Component parts for the display cabinet in Plate 41 are pictured in Plate 42 before being assembled. A set of desk pigeonholes (price, ten dollars) found hanging over a basement workbench at an estate sale is turned on end to become a display cabinet.

Note: This is one example of an "early-bird find"—arriving at eight-thirty when the sale opened, I bought the pigeonholes immediately, not waiting to examine other merchandise first. Although the piece looked shabby, with rough boards nailed on the back, drawers missing, etc., this is a type of sale item that dealers will buy if it's priced reasonably because it has potential and is partly oak.

Preliminary Steps. The pigeonholes and all supplementary parts were stripped of varnish (using TSP). Boards nailed to the back of the pigeonholes were eliminated—along with the single remaining drawer and two small shelf brackets, since these would reveal that the pigeonholes were meant to go the other way around.

Base. Preassembled table legs (half of a set) are used to support the compartmented display cabinet. The table leg's thick top board is replaced with an oak one, and wooden braces are added underneath it to reinforce the legs, thus creating a sturdy base.

Each end of the attractive curved board (shown in Plate 43, and used as a facing, or front apron, at the top of the legs) is cut in a miter box to a 45-degree angle. The side aprons, improvised from a piece of scrap oak joined to leftover ends of the front board, are also mitered. And so is part of the trim, devised by carefully shaping bits and

Plate 43: Base for cabinet in Plate 41.

pieces of carved oak (mostly saved from the board's sawed-off ends). The object is to make the side aprons appear to be a continuation of the fancy front-apron design.

This type of reconstruction is done a step at a time, and it's slow work, but fascinating. Small tools are needed (available from hardware stores; or Brookstone catalog, see list at end of Chapter 3): an X-acto knife with appropriate blades and sanding burrs, and your wood rasp and plenty of sandpaper. If the wood rasp is too rough, try a wood file instead (these are also available at hardware stores).

Top. Turning the pigeonholes on end left one side partially open. A board was cut and nailed in place to enclose this middle area. Also, since this side of the cabinet-to-be was in bad shape, a thin piece of veneered oak (from a bed panel) was glued and nailed to it, covering the entire side.

Because the molding-trimmed shelf board pictured in Plate 42 was not deep enough to serve as a cabinet top, a full-length, 4-inch-wide oak board was doweled and glued to it, giving it sufficient depth. The preassembled shelf was, however, longer than the cabinet by several inches, so the molding was removed from this excess and used to continue the trim around both ends of the top. An oiled finish enhances the antique look of the completed cabinet.

There are of course other things you can do with *all* of the materials recycled in these pieces (see Chapter 14, under "Variables"). But perhaps some of the ideas shown here may set you thinking of new imaginative ways to bring out your books and treasures and put them on dramatic display.

12

Dictionary/Reference-Book Stands

At the turn of the century, dictionary stands in ornate Victorian styles were made of brass or cast iron. The hinged flaps which held the book open or closed were rather creaky affairs whose hinges complained more with each passing year. As a result, rarely do you find one of these stands that has survived intact.

Nevertheless, a book stand continues to be a practical idea, one that today's decorators have taken to their hearts—as have furniture manufacturers who now produce a variety of styles ranging from quaint to modern.

You can build a book stand yourself that will suit your own individual needs and style of decor. One of the following designs, or a combination of ideas from all of them, could lead you into a new and fascinating area of creativity.

Styles of Book Stands

Whether you're constructing a freestanding floor model, a low stand to set on a desk, or a simple reading stand for newspaper or book, the one component common to all designs is a tilted top (book support) at the bottom of which is a ledge (book rest) to keep the book from sliding off.

Note: A more sophisticated stand might have a hinged book support that lies flat when not in use, with an adjustable brace (also hinged) to tilt the board to various angles.

Reading Stand

The reading stand in Plate 38 is made from the shaped back of a broken chair. Because it was split in two places, the oak chair back required gluing (with clamps applied until glue was dry) before it could be stripped of varnish. It also needed squaring off along the bottom edge so it would sit level without rocking.

Brace. The fold-back hinged brace is made from the leftover tip-end of the mirror easel in Plate 8. Existing curves of the easel were used to advantage in cutting out this piece. Further shaping was accomplished the same as for the coatrack in Chapter 2. (To enlarge pattern for the brace, Diagram 9b, follow instructions in Chapter 8, under "Rustic Desk.")

Note: If you have power tools available, you might wish to cut out a number of these braces—there's no end of material available for other parts of the stand. These stands would make fine gifts, or you might want to produce them as a saleable item.

Assembling Stand. A small brass hinge fastens the brace to back of stand (brace folds flat against back of stand when not in use). A two-part *elbow catch* is used to lock the brace into place when the reading stand is upright (Plate 44).

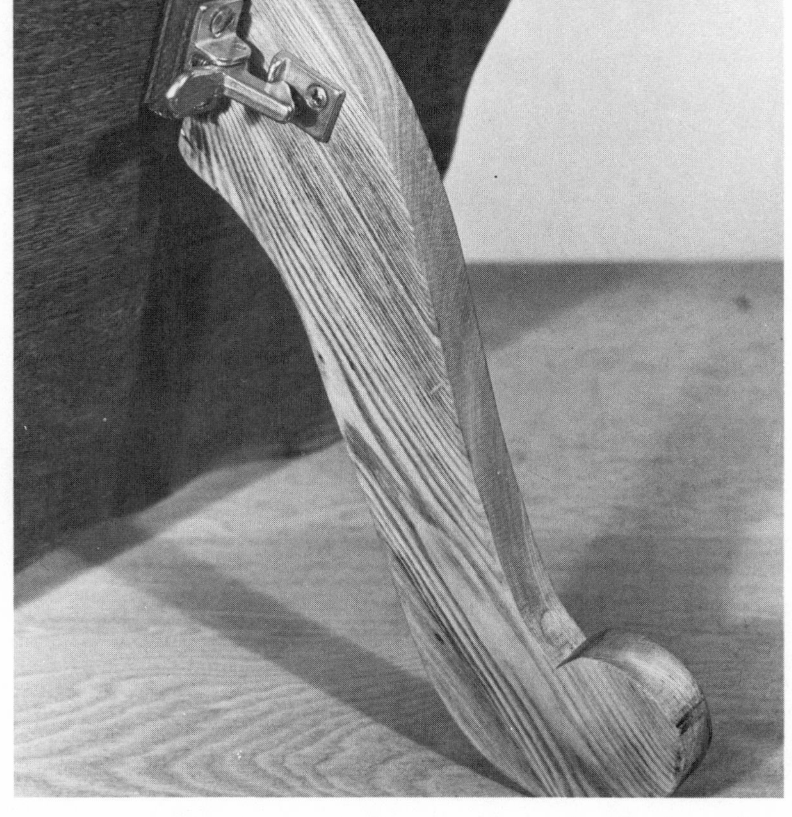

Plate 44: Enlarged view of elbow catch used to lock reading stand in upright position.

To install this type of catch, lay stand face down on table with the brace in upright position. Place catch on back of reading stand with the thumb-press area pointing outward and the point of catch touching the upright brace. With a pen or pencil mark points for drilling screw holes.

Next, cut a small wooden strip about the size of the catch; a scrap of ⅜-inch plywood will do. (In order to work smoothly, the catch must have a thin wood block inserted between it and the back of the stand. This will call for two screws that are longer than those provided in the elbow-catch package.)

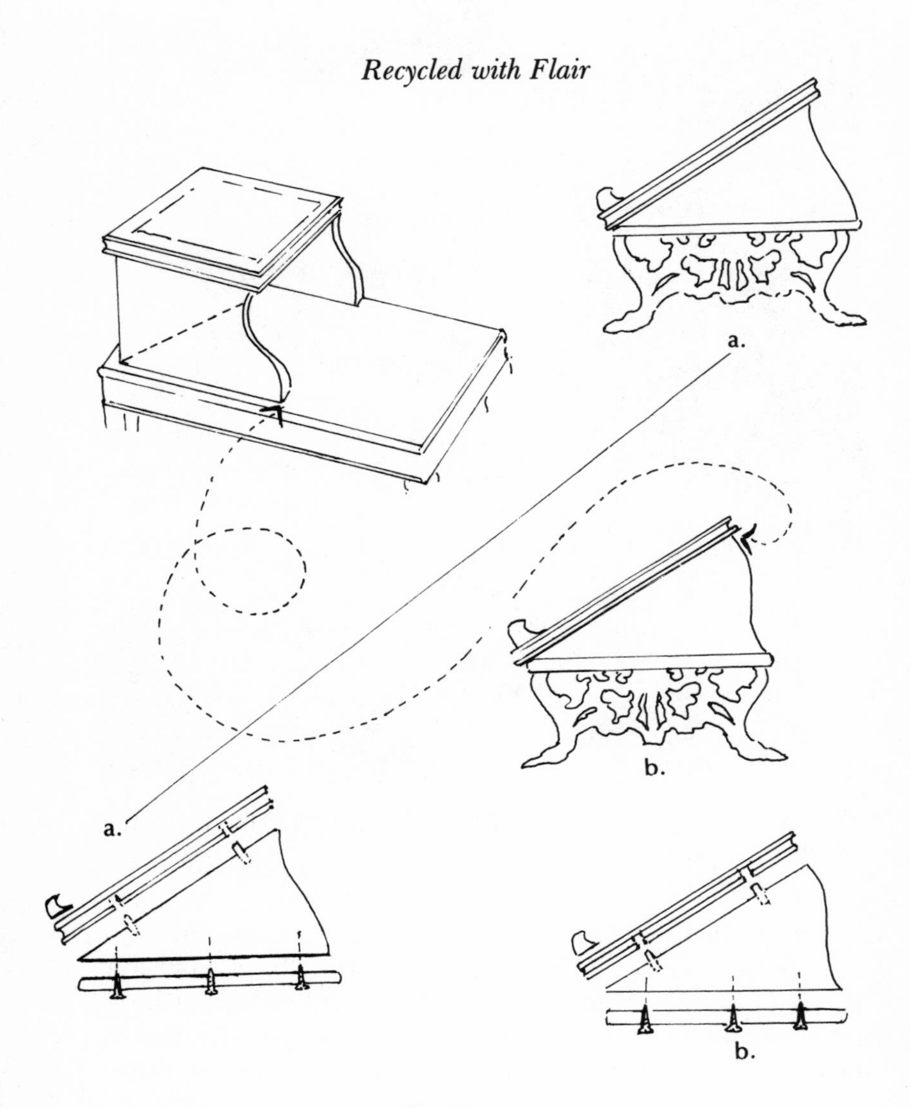

Diagram 13

Assemble (according to preference) as in a or b. Join bottom board to angled sides with screws, the tilted top with glue and wooden dowels. Glue book rest to top.

Mark and drill holes in this small piece of wood. Drill corresponding holes in back of stand. Set the catch on top of piece of wood, insert screws and tighten to fasten this part of the catch to the reading stand. Now mark location of screw holes on the brace for attaching the smaller strike-portion of the catch.

When both parts are in place, this neat little catch clicks into locking position or releases at the touch of your thumb.

Book Rest. The book rest is a narrow, 12-inch-long beveled board (of unknown origin) with an additional piece of molding—the same length as the book rest—glued underneath. (See Plate 38.)

Book Stand with Metal Legs

Legs. Ornate cast-iron legs—the base-portion of a worn-out footstool—become a handsome component for the stand in Plate 34.

Note: These legs could of course be used to support a newly upholstered footstool. And, since the book stand's top assembly is attached with four removable bolts through holes in the set of cast-iron legs, they may be recycled again with ease—on a footstool, or on a plant stand, for that matter.

Top Assembly. Two step-type end tables contribute wooden parts for the book-support section of the stand. The sturdy board topping the metal legs was a "step tread" salvaged from one table, while the angled sides of the book stand, as well as its tilted leather-covered top, are constructed from the step-assembly of another.

The "step" part of such a table cannot be tilted to serve as a book support without first disassembling it and cutting the sides to about a 45-degree angle (see Diagram 13)—or to whatever angle will tilt the book support to the

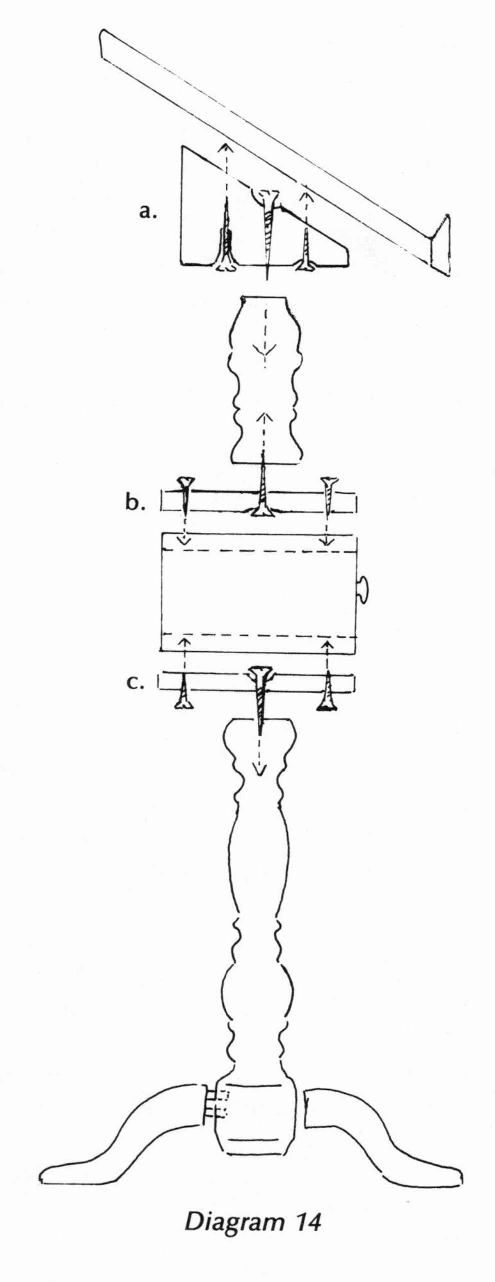

Diagram 14

Attach blocks a, b, and c to center post. Proceed as indicated in Chapter 12.

degree you wish; make a paper pattern, then cut accordingly. The curved-front "risers" that support the step and raise it a foot or more above the tabletop can then be utilized as sidepieces for the book stand. These are glued and doweled (using small-sized dowels) into the tilted top. The thick baseboard is attached with screws. A top of this type, incidentally, is ideal for recycling since it is preassembled and complete in itself, with a ¾-inch reinforced edge that makes it easy to work with.

The book rest, part of a picture frame, is attached to the leather-covered top (with screws from underneath) before wooden components of the book stand are assembled.

Tall Pedestal-Base Book Stand

Parts of two tables and a spice stand are converted into a floor-model book stand shown in Plate 3. This same design adapts well to a variety of bases, such as one from an old desk chair—the plant stand in Plate 29 which utilizes this type of base could easily be turned into a book stand by rebuilding it—inserting an angled block of wood underneath a tilted book-stand top, as illustrated in Diagram 14.

Assembling Stand. Use a preconstructed pedestal base, or dowel four curved supports into a central table leg, (see desk in Plate 4; Chapter 8). If a drawer, or drawers, are added midway attach an extra board of the same size to both top and bottom of the drawer-insert—for joining it to the pedestal, as shown in Diagram 14.

To attach the book-support board to the pedestal, an angled wooden block is fastened to the top section of the table leg with a large countersunk screw (Diagram 14a). *Before tightening this permanently, drill two holes in the wooden block for attaching the top.* These holes are drilled from underneath (straight side of the block) and the screw is countersunk to a depth of 1 inch or more where the block is thickest.

A thin scalloped book rest adds the finishing touch to this dictionary/reference-book stand.

Mrs. Fields, the antique dealer I told you about in Chapter 1, sells a good many of these stands in her shop. Her customers think they're both pretty and practical. And, says Mrs. Fields, the demand far exceeds the number she is able to supply.

Another case of reaching into the past for ideas that adapt well to today's living.

Part Three

The Finishing Touch

13

To Paint or Not to Paint

For quick conversion jobs—projects that require little or no rebuilding—paint is one kind of magic to consider. You can give secondhand furniture a first class look with nothing more than paint and imagination.

Stripping a painted or varnished piece down to the wood can be equally effective, as illustrated by the picture frame described in Chapter 5 (shown "before" in Plate 18 and "after" in Plate 19). More about this type of refinishing later.

When it comes to furniture that is made up of many parts from different sources, painting may be the only answer. But once you've completed renovation of a piece and are ready to paint, you discover it's decision time. What color? With so many beautiful choices, should you paint it turquoise, antiqued with gray? Would antique red look better? Or gold? Or green?

It is always easier to decide after you've put on a base coat. Why? Because this not only minimizes the distraction

Plate 45: Wall piece shown in Plate 5, prior to completion and before being painted.

of conflicting wood tones and puttied cover-ups, it brings into focus the overall design.

In fact it may be difficult to judge how well your various components blend until the entire piece is undercoated. For example, Plate 45 shows an assembled wallpiece before being given a base coat. After the piece was painted the undercoat served as a catalyst in pinpointing areas that looked unfinished, and additional trim was then applied to pull the design together, as illustrated in Plate 5.

Note: The way to add supplementary trim is to do it one step at a time—add a bit here, a piece there, then set your project up where you can study it while you work on something else. Try a variety of things but don't attach anything permanently until you hit on the right combination and the design "jells"—or you run across the type of trim you want.

Before we get into *color,* let's explore the possibilities in natural wood finishes.

Stripping, Sanding, Preparing the Wood

Unless your material is new, the first step will usually be stripping off previous coats of paint or varnish. For removing varnish, my favorite stripper is TSP, see below, under "Removers (Water Wash)." Paint may require a stronger agent.

Paint Removers (No-Wash)

Some paint removers do not require a washing of the surface after the softened paint or varnish has been scraped off. If you are working outdoors, or inside where ventilation is good, you may prefer a general purpose no-wash stripper.

Apply with a brush and leave the surface covered with

stripper for fifteen or twenty minutes. Then test with a scraper to see if paint or varnish is softened down to the wood. If so, scrape sludge away with a broad putty knife or spatula. For resistant areas apply a second coat of stripper and repeat procedure.

Removers (Solvent-Wash)

Other strippers require washing afterward with solvent. This type of remover leaves a waxy substance on the surface after the sludge is scraped away, and this must be removed with paint solvent or thinner before any kind of oil finish or varnish is applied.

Removers (Water-Wash)

(1) There is a jellied, semiliquid remover that works well for paint and is applied, then removed, the same way as no-wash removers except that a water wash is used afterward. If traces of finish remain, repeat procedure or use a follow-up application of hot TSP.

(2) TSP (trisodium phosphate) is a dry grainy powder—similar to sal soda—that you dissolve in hot water. This is used primarily for removing varnish. I find this method *most* satisfactory, but you'll need a driveway or some other place where you can quickly hose down the furniture afterward with cold water.

Note: A point to remember when buying packaged TSP. What you want is the old-fashioned kind. Don't buy one of the new fortified types; these are intended for *cleaning* only. (The label may read, "New improved formula" with added this or that. Whatever it is that they add seems to render it worthless for stripping.)

To Remove Varnish with TSP. If possible use an enameled pan. (An old canning kettle is just right, so watch for them at garage sales.) Heat to boiling two or three quarts of water (less if you're stripping small items); carry outside before adding TSP as it may cause liquid to bubble over the top. Make the solution quite strong, using over half a pound of TSP and, as the water cools, put in more boiling water (and more TSP if necessary).

Wear rubber gloves and use a handled brush to slop the hot liquid generously over the object you are stripping. Work fast. Wet down the entire area to be stripped as quickly as possible. Avoid leaving any dry places on the wood—TSP has a slight bleaching action, and dry spots will leave a line of demarcation, causing the wood to look streaked after the wet-down areas have dried.

The first time the solution is applied, you may doubt it's doing the job, but slop on more liquid with the brush, and in a few minutes you'll see the varnish letting go. Scrub the whole thing down several times, working quickly so the water stays hot. Then hose with cold water using a nozzle to get more pressure. Remove excess moisture with a rag or an old towel.

Note: If you happen to be out of TSP, plain sal soda used the same way will do a passable job of *varnish* stripping. Just be sure to make a fairly strong solution and keep it hot.

After the piece has dried enough for you to see places you've missed, sand these down, or wait until the furniture is dry and repeat the stripping process. (If you do it again immediately while the piece is very wet, the stripping action is lessened.)

Ideally, the time to do this type of stripping is on a warm day in the sun. But don't leave furniture in direct sunlight to dry. Wipe off excess moisture, move piece into a cool dry place and allow several days to a week for further drying before adding the finish.

One more point. After a board or piece of furniture has

been stripped down completely, don't let it dry out over a long period of time—the wood may split or crack, particularly if it is old. To restore moisture to the wood apply a mixture of half turpentine and half boiled linseed oil, then wipe thoroughly with a rag.

Stripping Problems

Plastic Finishes and Gesso

Be careful about buying painted and antiqued furniture that has been coated with a plastic finish such as Varathane if you plan to have it commercially stripped—most commercial strippers will not guarantee results, and some refuse plastic-finished furniture altogether.

Gesso undercoating cannot be stripped off.

Carved Areas or Indentations

When stripping pieces with carving or deep grooves, it is often necessary to use a knife, chisel or screwdriver to clean out depressions where varnish or paint has collected more thickly.

To Strip Small Carved or Pressed-Wood Ornaments. Apply remover (solvent-wash or water-wash), remove sludge, clean well, use steel wool and sandpaper. Also, scrape old glue off back of ornaments while wet.

Or let ornaments soak for a half hour or longer in hot TSP solution, rinse in clear water, dry between paper towels, remove any remaining paint or varnish in cracks or grooves. Finally, whatever agent you employ to strip them, to avoid warping, place ornaments carefully between two boards and clamp boards lightly in vise until ornaments are dry.

Note: It's a good idea to strip a number of these small wooden pieces at the same time. This will give you a good backlog of finishing material that is ready when you need it.

Red Mahogany Stain

No amount of stripping or bleaching will completely remove this color of stain; the wood simply turns pink. Even when it has been stripped, the color may bleed through future coats of paint. To eliminate the problem, seal in any leftover stain with low gloss varnish and let it dry before adding a base coat of paint.

Dark Spots in the Wood

If dark stained areas remain after paint or varnish is removed, use a two-part bleaching solution (available in paint stores). This works well in some cases unless the stain is very deep. For more on this, see "Bleaching," this chapter.

Stains and Wood Finishes

There are various schools of thought on the subject of furniture finishing. And also some excellent books.* Depending on the type of finish you prefer, the process can be as simple or as sophisticated and painstaking as you wish to make it.

I favor a natural, rubbed finish rather than a high-gloss one, and since most of the pieces in this book are done in this fashion, we'll deal here only with the simplest methods for finishing furniture to bring out the natural wood grain.

Note: Woods such as cedar or fir may appear dull and lifeless if simply treated with oil. Even when all components are well matched and require no color blending, a coat of satin-finish varnish often adds just enough luster to make this type of wood look finished and attractive.

---

*Two of these are: *Complete Book of Furniture Repair and Refinishing* by Ralph Parsons Kinney, Scribner's, 1971, and *The Furniture Doctor* by George Grotz, Doubleday, 1962.

(Some brands of satin-finish varnish are glossier than others and produce a too-shiny finish, so buy a small can at first.)

Oil Stains

You can buy stains that are opaque or clear. I favor clear ones as a rule, but sometimes use opaque to get a deeper color, wiping it off almost immediately.

Wood Tones (Selecting the Right Stain). It is a good idea to have several small cans of wood stain on hand in various colors. For instance, dark oak or Spanish oak (on the brownish or black side), golden oak (into the yellow tones), Salem or Colonial maple (reddish). I like to mix them to get the color I want for a particular piece—but *never* mix an opaque stain with a clear one. It seems to me that the golden oaks are apt to be a bit too yellow and need a touch of brown or red, and most other colors seem to benefit from small alterations as well. On a shelf near my workbench, I store five or six colors and when a new one is needed, open two or three colors, mix together a little of each in a tin can, then pour the mixture into a container with a lid for storing. Eventually this expands your range of colors.

Along with your collection of stains, keep a jar of boiled linseed oil and turpentine (see "Formulas," this chapter). You may want to use this mixture before staining raw woods (old oak, particularly) to see how much color the wood will show. Incidentally, you can put this on, wipe well and add stain immediately if more color is needed.

Note: Save tin cans, jar lids, etc., wash well and stow them near your workbench to use as containers for paint, stain, bleach, and thinner for soaking brushes. A piece of foil over the top works fine as a cover.

And be sure to collect soft, lintless rags. They are a necessity for all types of furniture finishing.

Formulas

This is my version (a simplified one) of a favorite finish for old wood and antiques.

Linseed Oil and Turpentine

Pour equal amounts of boiled linseed oil and turpentine or thinner into a jar. Paint or wipe the mixture onto sanded-smooth raw wood. (For large pieces of furniture, do one section at a time.) But first be sure there are no remaining traces of varnish on the wood, or the oil will not soak in. Also, go over surfaces with a tack rag to remove traces of sawdust and lint.

Wipe well, almost immediately, until the oil disappears from the surface, going over the wood a final time with the palm of your hand or a tack rag, to pick up any lint.

Do not varnish or wax, but simply repeat the oiling treatment from time to time—in a week, a month or whenever it seems desirable. This reoiling process can be continued indefinitely. Or when the wood is exactly to your liking, seal it at any time with varnish and call it done.

There are rewards in using this type of finish. The oil adds life to the wood and also protects it. Best of all, you can introduce immediately into your decorating scheme a piece of furniture you've just oiled, without waiting for lengthy finishing procedures.

Another advantage: scratches or mars can be touched up whenever you wish, so long as you don't add varnish or a sealer—just sand, then reoil. It makes no difference if the marks are old ones or scars that your furniture acquired today.

Traditionally, a linseed oil finish is "built up" by rubbing the oil mixture into the wood with the palm of your hand or a soft rag once a week for *six months.* Personally, I haven't the patience, although I've occasionally applied linseed oil to an unvarnished oak table that has been in our family for years, and each time I do, it takes on new life and beauty.

Note: After the first application, you may prefer to add a bit more oil in ratio to the turpentine. (I like a thin half-and-half mixture because it dries more quickly, with no stickiness.)

Following are two present-day interpretations of old formulas for refinishing wood—the first, a paint-on, wipe-off stain; the second, a rubbed beeswax finish. Both are excellent for pine.

Formula for Stain (Grace Gray's Version)

2 cups (1 pint) turpentine
1 tablespoon raw (unboiled) linseed oil
½ tablespoon burnt umber (artists' oil color)
¾ teaspoon walnut stain

Mix well. Paint on, wipe off and allow wood to dry. (Stir mixture before using again.) The picture frame in Plate 12 is finished in this manner.

Beeswax Finish (Del Smith's)

Proportions not critical—but start with:
1 pound beeswax
1 pint linseed oil (original recipe calls for raw, but he has always used boiled)
Turpentine (about one-third as much turpentine as oil)
½ teaspoon burnt umber oil color (approximately)

Melt beeswax in coffee can (set in pan of water over low heat). As soon as wax melts take outside (it is flammable) and add linseed oil. Mixture tends to stiffen—may need to be set in pan of hot water again. If mixture gets too stiff add more oil or turpentine.

This can be kept for some time in a covered can. If it forms a scum, melt down and strain for reuse.

Antiquing Mixture

See "Antiquing a Varnished Wood Surface" in this chapter.

Different Effects

To Highlight a Natural Finish. Rub piece with superfine 4/0 (0000) steel wool to lighten finish in raised areas.

For New Wood. Apply Danish oil (natural or with stain in it), sand, add another coat of oil, then Trewax paste wax, and rub with superfine steel wool.

Cover-Ups. See Chapter 5, "Spanish Frame," also "Antiquing Touch-Ups" in this chapter.

Distressed Wood Finish. Since the idea here is to mellow the finish and make it appear aged, you must start with a battered surface, not a smooth one. To accomplish this, use a wooden mallet, a length of chain, odd shaped pieces of metal or a ball-peen hammer to "distress" the wood before it is painted.

The antiquing mixture then settles into the dents, mars and scratches you've created, giving the finish a used and ancient look.

Contrasting Woods. When it comes to wood trim, you may occasionally prefer a contrast of tones. You might, for example, trim a light-toned chest with wooden handles and molding in a darker shade.

How to Make Woods Match

Bleaching

To bleach small pieces of wood such as ornamental trim, pour equal amounts of two-part bleaching solution—part one and part two—into shallow containers and soak the pieces for a few minutes in each. Remove and rinse in clear water. Dry with paper towels and press between two boards until dry.

For bleaching larger areas, mix parts one and two as directed, brush quickly on surface and allow to remain a few minutes (until the wood starts turning lighter). Rinse immediately with cold water. You may also want to try using a household bleach (though I never have), diluting as directed and using the methods described above.

Example: Candleholder Frame. Suppose you've assembled a variety of wooden parts salvaged from many places. Even if they are all of the same kind of wood they may vary as to tone, ranging from dark to light. Or they may be of different kinds of wood.

The component parts of the candleholder frame in Plate 19, Chapter 5, are an example. The brackets used for this frame had been painted black and retained some traces of this charcoal tone even after being stripped. The candle cups (salt and pepper shaker tops) had been stained and were an in-between shade. Thus, neither brackets nor candle cups matched the light oak of the frame.

First, brackets and cups were stripped with TSP, which tends to bleach wood. The brackets came out the right color except for a few areas where the flat black paint still showed. This was mostly surface color—not penetrating into the grain of the wood. Sanding removed these touches of black.

The shaker tops, which had retained a good deal of wood stain, were dropped into a bleaching solution for a few minutes, then rinsed with water. The ornamental corner pieces also needed bleaching as they were a darker wood than the frame.

Pull It Together with Antiquing.

Staining a combination of different woods darker in order to blend them doesn't always work since each wood absorbs differently.

Example: Bulletin Board Frame. The bulletin board with posts and shelf in Plate 17, Chapter 5, is assembled from woods of varying shades. Instead of using bleach to unify the wood tones, they are blended with antiquing applied over a coat of satin-finish varnish. This works well for woods that don't take stain well and is sometimes all that is needed to pull a composite piece together.

Note: The reason for varnishing before antiquing is that raw woods soak up too much color in some places, not enough in others, and results can be spotty or uneven. A coat of varnish prevents antiquing stain from soaking into the wood, gives you time to wipe it off or blend and shade it to your satisfaction.

To ensure complete coverage with varnish on a frame or wall piece of this type, do the components—posts, frame, shelf—separately before they are permanently assembled (but not until holes have been drilled, screws tested for length, size, etc.)

Allow varnish to dry thoroughly then, before you antique, brush on another light coat after all the components are fastened together, taking care to varnish around assembly areas and over hole plugs that have been added and so on.

Antiquing a Varnished Wood Surface

To Apply Antiquing Mixture. Basic antiquing liquid consists of equal parts burnt umber (see below) and turpentine or paint thinner. Start with a tablespoon or two of each. Squeeze oil color from tube onto a plate or shallow pan. Add approximately same amount of thinner and mix thoroughly with a palette knife.

Note: When you buy burnt umber (or other artists' oil colors), the shade will vary a trifle from one brand to another. For example, Grumbacher's burnt umber is dark and definitely brown; Malfa's is a warmer red-toned brown; Shiva burnt umber has a greenish, olive cast.

Apply the dark mixture with a brush, covering surface completely. Allow to set for a few minutes until the shine disappears, then start wiping with a soft lintless rag—an old silk head scarf cut into pieces is good.

For contrast, allow deeper places and indentations to remain dark, but pick up any heavy residues of antiquing liquid with a soft, dry brush. Using a small piece of cloth, pat to blend light and dark areas, but work quickly. Try not to go over any one place more than absolutely necessary. Do not touch freshly antiqued areas until after they're varnished as every fingerprint will show.

Highlight rounded portions of posts by wiping off more of the color.

Final Varnishing. With any natural finish that shows the grain of the wood—whether it is antiqued or not—you may want to add a light coat of varnish for durability. Of course if antiquing has been done, let it dry *at least* twenty-four hours before you varnish.

Additional coats of varnish are optional. Those who do tole or other decorative painting apply several protective coats of a plastic finish such as Varathane (beginning forty-eight hours or more after a design is completed), then a final coat of low gloss varnish.

Lint ruins more varnish jobs than any other one thing,

so save your varnishing for a quiet time—avoid doing it when the family is moving about or the dryer is on.

Do not shake varnish can; stir gently from the bottom and set can in a pan of warm water. Wipe surfaces to be coated with palm of hand or tack rag, then flow on warm varnish in one direction using a brush that is reserved for varnishing only—one with light bristles, since black ones sometimes discolor the varnish.

Color

A word about decorative painting. Since this is a special field in itself, we won't go into techniques except to say it's a craft that is unusually compatible with this type of do-it-yourself rebuilding.

A prime example is Betty Breitbarth's mix-and-match cupboard in Plate 2. The deep olive tone of the cupboard sets off the four colorful designs. Without them, this large a piece of furniture might appear too dark. As a rule when you intend to antique—unless you're doing an almost-black accent piece such as this—choose a bright, clear background color: the brighter the color the better it will antique.

Antiquing Over Paint

Use semi-gloss or satin-finish paint on any surface that you plan to antique. A color that is too flat, or one that is high gloss, must be coated with satin-finish varnish and allowed to dry for twenty-four hours before it is antiqued.

For antiquing a painted surface, follow same method used in "Antiquing a Varnished Wood Surface" (this chapter).

Distressed Finish (Color). See instructions under "Distressed Wood Finish" (this chapter). Two colors that lend themselves well to this type of finish are antique red (vermilion, antiqued with burnt umber) and Swedish blue (use a good bright blue, the color of Dutch tiles, antiqued with raw umber and a dash of Payne's grey).

Antiquing in Stages

If you're doing a very large piece or an intricate one that requires extra time and attention, don't antique the whole thing at once—break the operation into two or more easy stages. (Cupboards are usually done in two stages: first the outside, then the inside.)

Note: An alternative method is to have someone help you by applying the antiquing liquid while you follow behind wiping and blending.

Example: Doll Bed. The canopy doll bed in Plates 15 and 16 has a natural wood finish, so let's assume you're going to antique a painted four-poster constructed utilizing an upside-down table as in Diagram 3a. The first step consists of antiquing the four posts and the headboard. These are allowed to dry, then coated with satin-finish varnish.

In step two, the main portion of the bed is antiqued and—after it is dry—varnished.

Note: When you antique in stages, always do first the parts that will be most exposed to view after they're done. Because once these areas have been protected with varnish, fingerprints or spatters can simply be wiped off as you proceed with stage two. Also, runs or slight imperfections (where the two stages meet) will be less apt to show.

First stage: Remove mattress board. Antique this separately, completing one side of the board in stage one, the other in stage two.

Rest bed securely on a box or table where you can walk around the bed and see it from all angles, and so that its feet are accessible for antiquing. Paint with antiquing mixture the bed's four feet, the posts and the headboard. When the shine disappears (ten minutes, more or less) start wiping—begin with posts at head of bed, starting at top and working down.

Check posts from all sides as you pat and blend (with a soft folded rag) to be sure there are no dark, unwiped areas you've overlooked.

Next, wipe the antiquing off the other two posts. Now comes the headboard. To do this, wipe with a long sweeping stroke across the board from one side to the other, stopping short of the posts on either side. Then do the feet, using the same procedure described for the posts.

Leave dark shaded areas where posts intersect headboard, but pick up any thick deposits of antiquing mixture here and in corners with a soft, dry brush.

Pat to blend—*quickly* with a minimal amount of reworking. Carefully wipe off dark spatters or runs on main body of the bed so surface will be receptive to antiquing mixture when you do this area in the second stage.

Let antiquing dry twenty-four hours or more, then varnish with satin-finish varnish. (See "Final Varnishing," under "Antiquing a Varnished Wood Surface," this chapter.)

Second stage: When varnish has dried on "stage one," apply antiquing to rest of bed, wait a few minutes, then wipe it off with long quick strokes. Be sure to clean any runs or spatters off the already varnished stage one—use a clean rag or Q-tips dampened with turpentine or thinner. Repeat drying and varnishing process as before.

Antiquing Touch-Ups. Should you discover a few tiny spots you've missed after a piece is completely antiqued and varnished, do this: Put a dab of burnt umber oil color, and a half teaspoon or less of varnish in a jar lid. (Don't mix.) Using a very small brush, apply first umber then varnish to the spot, blending with the tip of your finger. This method is also effective for repairing small chips or damaged areas on antiqued furniture that is beginning to show wear.

When the time comes for finishing don't be afraid to experiment! Wood tones or color can highlight a project's best features, give it simplicity and style. A natural finish or a painted one—both are marvelous factors for enhancing your furniture's design.

14

A Little Imagination—with Economy in Mind

Not too long ago, matched sets—from chairs to china—were the thing. Today variety and individuality are often more highly prized. When you are hunting for antique or near-antique furniture, look for remainders of sets. The leftover unmatched pieces are the hardy survivors and usually the best bargains. A matched set of dining chairs, for instance, is often priced out of sight. But do you really want a *set*? With individuality the keynote, why not aim for variety but tie your chairs or collectibles together according to color or category. For example, oak pressed-back chairs could be acquired one at a time, each with back and rungs of different design. If they aren't solid-seated chairs, and you don't want the expense of having them caned, upholster all of the seats in the same fabric.

Note: To do this buy some upholstery webbing or burlap

at an upholstery store. Turn the chair over and tack webbing or burlap to the underside of the chair seat. Cut 1½-inch thick foam rubber to fit in open space in seat (this is supported by the webbing or burlap). Lay your chair seat fabric flat (don't turn the edge under). Tack fabric securely to the chair with ⅜-inch upholstery tacks; use plenty. Glue braid over fabric edge with Elmer's Glue-All (white all-purpose glue).

One-of-a-Kind Accessories

The mix and match approach can be employed when hunting for bargain-priced accessories too. For instance, single pieces of elegant china that once belonged to a beautiful set—a gravy boat, or a sugar bowl without a lid—can be used for dried arrangements or fresh flowers, or on a desk to hold pens and pencils. It's also agreeable to adapt these less expensive one of a kinds for table settings. If you collect singles, make your objective a mixed bag of shapes and patterns in just one (or perhaps two) colors. Zero in on a favorite color—say, pink—pink dinner plates. Consider a mix of patterned and plain. Or perhaps you prefer blue and white—try cups with complementary saucers instead of matching ones. A white saucer with a blue cup, or a figured cup with a plain saucer and so on. Use your imagination! It's a fact that unrelated objects placed in the right surroundings suddenly become compatible. And therein lies the fun!

A special table setting calls for a special background. Table linens present a challenge because a fresh and attractive secondhand tablecloth is the exception, not the rule. (Though estate sales may surprise you with elegant antique cloths.) So when you're in the market for table coverings, the trick is to "think tablecloth" (and napkins) when you look at any handsome fabric—be it draperies,

Plate 46: Centerpiece arrangement by the author, using candlelight and old glass.

upholstery material, a bedspread or simply a length of new fabric, printed or plain. For a fabulous effect, put a dark-background print under lighter-toned dishes.

For a spectacular centerpiece when entertaining guests at dinner, use glass dishes (vintage or otherwise) as illustrated in Plate 46. Glass pieces in the photo (bought at garage and estate sales over a period of time) are antique celery dishes, sugar bowls and odds and ends of decorative glass of varying heights, each one exquisitely cut or shaped in a different design.

Shown here grouped on a garage sale mirror, they shimmer in a glow of light cast by floating wicks.* The fairyland-at-night effect is enhanced by reflections in the mirrored base.

Note: An inexpensive secondhand mirror such as this one, or even a new one from the dime store, will produce nearly as glamorous a showing if you group on it an assortment of ordinary vigil candles in their glass cups, either clear or colored ones, with perhaps a tall glass candlestick or two for height—or use whatever you happen to have in glassware. It is primarily the mirror's dramatic enhancement of candlelight by reflection that makes this type of centerpiece so attractive.

Make Assets of the Things You Collect—
Or Things You Have

Some accessories and antiques have no real place in today's living. But instead of packing them away, why not use old things in new or different ways? One woman told me how she adapted a silver sugar bowl (the kind with brackets around the edge that once held a set of teaspoons).

It is now a charming accent on a dressing table in her daughters' bath; the footed bowl holds tubes of toothpaste, while the girls' bright-handled toothbrushes hang suspended from its silver rim.

A dressing table, by the way, is a perfect setting for cherished accessory finds—a delightful place to put me-

---

*Pick-a-wick by Corning. Safe, inexpensive, "Un-Candles"; wicks designed to float while lighted, on water plus 2 inches of any vegetable oil.

Ordinary candles of appropriate sizes can of course be used instead.

mentos or small collectibles that bring you pleasure—such as a covered dish with roses painted on the lid, a miniature frame (possibly found in church rummage) or an antique glass (to hold spring violets). A thrift store box, a garage sale tray—junking's a fine way to acquire quality accessories at minimal cost.

Fortunately, tastes differ; one person's junk is another's treasure. And there's no explaining why any of us buy the particular things that we do.

Among the small collectibles I find appealing are cast-iron wall spindles (from the rolltop desk era). Their bases are usually painted black or dark green, and are basically oval in shape, cast in a variety of embossed, openwork designs. They are 3 to 4 inches high, with an upward-curving spike for impaling bills, receipts, letters and such—great for corralling papers that you want to save, yet quickly find again without delving into drawers or boxes. I use them in various ways and hang at least one in practically every room in the house.

One of these little spindles—minus the papers—also makes an attractive hanger for a small picture or some other ornamental object such as a cast-iron matchbox. By combining the small matchbox and the spindle, each lends importance to the other, creating a larger, more decorative accessory.

The hanging planters in Plate 47 are assembled from a collection of single brass parts and lighting fixture pieces (acquired at various sales). These are fastened together with hexagon nuts and two short lengths of threaded lamp rod.

Do you have glass prisms from a long-ago lamp tucked away in a drawer somewhere? Buy a few long prism pins at a lamp shop or use fine wire to hang the prisms on a planter and enjoy seeing them sparkle in the sunlight.

Plate 47: Hanging planters (with prisms) assembled by the author from metal parts.

Refurbish or Rebuild? The Easier Way

It is always a pleasure when you find secondhand furniture that needs little or no rebuilding but merely a fresh new look and perhaps a few supplementary parts.

With this kind of piece, while remodeling offers a challenge, there's an easier path you can follow. For example, neither the elegant trim nor the base is essential to the bookcase in Plate 40. The top portion alone would make an acceptable piece of furniture simply by adding shelves and repairing the back of the bookcase.

And the phonograph cabinet utilized for the composite piece in Plate 10 might be recycled with a minimum of time, effort and material simply by replacing its missing top and doors, then using it to house stereo equipment. Incidentally, the easiest method of all for refurbishing drab or shabby furniture is a spray painted finish similar to that used on this old cabinet.

Note: Satin black spray paint not only emphasizes with dramatic effect an accent piece of furniture, it will pick up and enhance any dark-toned accessories in the room as well.

To my way of thinking, some furniture relics do not merit the work and expense needed to restore them to their original state. For example, though tables that have beautifully shaped and beveled tops or turned legs with claw-and-ball feet or ornate moldings are of course collectible and well worth refinishing, you will seldom find a small table of this type that isn't wobbly to some degree. They are also particularly difficult to strengthen or reinforce, and the sprawling legs are toe catchers, which is porbably why so many of these tables are found with legs broken or mended.

Tops of these better-quality tables (that have weak or damaged legs) may be unusually handsome, and setting the top on a pedestal base is an easy way to improve both looks and practicality.

New Materials

The partial listing of *new* products for the do-it-yourselfer, in Chapter 3, gives only a glimpse of their potential as building aids and creative material. In addition to hardwood posts and splendid wood turnings, there are many synthetic products. The most fascinating feature of today's plastic materials, in regard to texture, graining, color and so on, is their uncanny resemblance to the real thing.

For this reason, as well as economy, you can supplement almost any style of decor with a do-it-yourself piece that utilizes one or more synthetic materials.

Note: The principal fun in working with plastic products is being able to adapt them in creative ways to suit individual tastes or ideas. For instance, you might want to saw apart and apply as ornamentation, the (4 inch by 10 inch) sections of imitation carved wood that are basically designed as backing and trim for shelf-installation strips.

Happily, these synthetic materials have alternative uses. In fact this is a low-cost way to supplement your decorative accessories and is quite acceptable on an accent piece of furniture for *effect* or to create a particular mood.

While assembly-line plastic or wood products may not produce the highest quality furniture and accessories, rest assured the projects you build with them *can* be unique, being of your own design.

By the way, you are apt to find this type of new material

Plate 48: An alternative design by Betty Breitbarth, the desk/buffet in Plate 12 is shown here set on cast-iron legs from an old sewing machine.

(often still in the package) at garage, estate or fund-raising sales for a fraction of the original cost.

Variables

The same pieces need not always produce the same end result. For example, the wall-hung desk/buffet in Plate 12 is shown in Plate 48 set on cast-iron legs salvaged from an old sewing machine.

The pigeonholed display cabinet in Plate 41 could of course be turned right side up and supported by heavy brackets or simply hung on the wall. It might be used to top a large desk, a long chest or an old table, and its appearance would be altered completely, depending on how it's adapted and what it contains.

To summarize, look for changeable elements in secondhand pieces of furniture. Picture them plus or minus a part or two, repainted, cut in half, made taller, stripped down, dressed up, turned on end or with different legs and another top.

In the marketplace of antiques and secondhands, patience is the watchword—what you don't find today, you may find tomorrow. It's a world crammed with choices, where anyone who takes the time to shop can run down excellent buys. *If the price is right and you like it, it's a bargain.* Never mind what other people collect; trust your own taste.

You never know when a lightning idea will strike! Or you'll find the bargain of the year! In the meantime, create your own happy environment surrounded by things you like and are truly comfortable with. That's what home is all about.